TRUST ME: AI RISK MANAGEMENT

RISK-CONTROLS FOR AI ASSURANCE AND ACCOUNTABILITY

Gregory Hutchins PE CERM

Margaux Hutchins

© 2024 by Gregory Hutchins PE CERM & Margaux Hutchins

Working It®; 7P's™; Work Lesson Earned™; VUCAN®, Proactive, Preventive, Predictive, and Preemptive®; CERM: AI risk-based, Problem-solving | AI risk-based, Decision-making® are trademarks of Quality Plus Engineering.

All rights reserved. No part of this book can be reproduced or transmitted in any form or by any means, electronic or mechanical, including photocopying, recording, or by any information storage or retrieval system without written permission from Quality Plus Engineering, except for the inclusion of quotations in a review. No patent or trademark liability is assumed with respect to the use of information contained in this book. Every precaution has been taken in the preparation of **Trust Me: AI Risk Management**. The publisher and author assume no responsibility for damages resulting from the use of information herein.

All brand names, trademarks and intellectual property belong to their respective holders. This publication contains the opinions and ideas of its author. It is intended to give helpful and informative material on the subject matter covered. It is sold with the understanding the author and publisher are not engaged in rendering professional services in this book. If the reader requires personal assistance or advice, a competent professional be consulted.

Note: Trust Me: AI Risk Management is based on original content. Sections of the book were edited using Chat: GPT and Bard.

Disclaimer: The author and publisher specifically refuse any responsibility for any liability, loss, and AI risk, personal or otherwise, which is incurred consequently, directly, or indirectly, of the use and application of any of the contents of this book. If further assistance is required, please seek the assistance of a career, physician, or other healthcare professional.

TABLE OF CONTENTS

Topic	Page
Introduction	7
AI Uncertainty	17
ISO 31000 Risk Management Principles	41
ISO 31000 Risk Management Framework	61
AI Risk Principles	79
AI First Enterprise	101
AI Governance	117
AI Context	131
AI Risk Assessment	143
AI Risk Appetite	169
AI Risk Treatment	183
AI Conformity Assessment	197
AI Futures	219

INTRODUCTION

WHAT IS THE KEY IDEA IN THIS CHAPTER?

In our global economy, trust is a fundamental requirement. Humans fly because humans trust the Federal Aviation Administration (U.S.) to inspect and approve plane manufacturers, verify pilots are trained and certified, and review air carrier procedures. This is the same for food and pharmaceutical products and frankly for most if not all things humans do from driving, flying, and almost everything. So, what do humans do with AI when most of the world's problem-solving and even decision-making will be done through autonomous machines?

TRUST ME: AI RISK MANAGEMENT

This book covers the following AI risk management and risk-controls material:

- **Introduction:** In our global economy, trust is a fundamental requirement. So, what do humans do with AI when most of the world's problem-solving and even risk-based, decision-making will be done through autonomous machines?

- **AI Uncertainty:** Uncertainty is today's 'new normal' in a world due to the complex and rapidly changing nature of our interconnected world. Navigating this uncertainty requires adaptability, resilience, and the ability to make risk-based decisions in the face of incomplete information.

- **ISO 31000 Risk Management Principles:** ISO 31000 is a risk management standard for the process of identifying, assessing, and managing risks. Risks are things that can go wrong and cause harm to an enterprise. ISO 31000 risk management is important because it helps companies to avoid or reduce the impact of risks.

- **ISO 31000 Risk Management Framework:** Risk management framework is a set of processes and procedures that helps companies to identify, assess, and manage risks. The purpose of an ISO 31000 risk management framework is to help companies to make risk-based decisions and assure accountable and safe AI.

- **AI Risk Principles:** AI trust involves many of its characteristics that are based on context. In this chapter, many elements of trust are discussed including: fairness, safety, privacy, robustness, transparency, environmental friendliness, traceability, and maintainability.

- **AI First Enterprise:** Every company will shortly become an AI enterprise. An AI enterprise is a company that is focused on the development and use of AI. AI companies are found in a variety of industries including healthcare, finance, and manufacturing.

- **AI Governance:** AI governance is the risk management framework, risk processes, and risk policies put in place to assure responsible and ethical AI development, deployment, and use of systems.

- **AI Context:** AI context includes the environment and stakeholders involved in AI development and use. These include AI developers, users, and other impacted humans.

- **AI Risk Assessment:** AI risk assessment is the process of identifying, evaluating, and analyzing potential AI system risks. It involves examining the risks posed by AI technologies to understand their risk likelihood and potential consequences for various stakeholders, systems, and organizations. AI risk assessment involves three elements: 1. Identify AI risks; 2. Evaluate AI risks; and 3. Analyze AI risks.

- **AI Risk Appetite:** AI risk appetite is an organization's willingness to accept and tolerate certain levels of risk with the development, deployment, and use of AI systems. Or expressed in another way, it represents the extent to which an organization is willing to take on risks in pursuit of its AI objectives.

- **AI Risk Treatment:** AI risk treatment is the process of implementing measures, risk-controls, and actions to manage, mitigate, or control risks with AI systems. Risk treatment measures will depend on the nature of the AI system, the identified

Introduction

risks, the organization's risk appetite, regulatory requirements, and ethical considerations.

- **AI Conformity Assessment:** AI conformity assessment is a process of evaluating whether an AI system complies with relevant laws, regulations, and technical standards. Conformity assessment is the basis for trusting AI software and systems. It is an important part of any enterprise's AI risk management program and framework.

- **AI Futures:** AI involves many present and future challenges.

ORGANIZATION OF BOOK

Each section of the book is organized in terms of three headers:

1. What is the risk?
2. What are AI risk-control examples?
3. Why it matters?

WHAT IS THE RISK?

AI risk is the likelihood and consequence of some harm to possibly occurring to humans, property, and other areas. Our approach to managing AI risk is to focus on risk-based, problem-solving and decision-making based on ISO risk management frameworks such as ISO 31000. We also emphasize the context and various elements of AI risk.

WHAT ARE AI RISK-CONTROL EXAMPLES?

AI risk-control is the process of identifying, analyzing, evaluating, and mitigating risks of AI systems.[1] This is book is based on our trademarked Proactive, Preventive, Predictive, and Preemptive® and Architect, Design, Deploy, and Assure® approaches to AI risk management.

WHY IT MATTERS?

Each section in this book ends with 'Why It Matters.' It explains and even reiterates why a certain topic is important for the risk management of AI.

'TRUST ME' BOOK SERIES

Trust is essential when it comes to AI. That is why we created a new series of books called 'Trust Me'.

WHAT IS THE RISK?

As the title of this book says: Trust Me is an important topic in AI. Many would say that it is now the most important topic in AI right now. IBM recently posed this question: 'What level of trust can – and should 'we place in AI systems?'[2]

A Google engineer recently mentioned that AI could be sentient. This caused a furor. He was immediately terminated. Why? Fear? Too close to the truth? Humans do not really know. What millions now know about AI from using ChatGPT and other chatbots is the technology seems eerily human.

This brings up the next important question: 'Can humans try to instill human values into AI?' AI already seems to be getting personal as it becomes pervasive in autonomous risk-based, problem-solving and decision-making.

WHAT ARE AI RISK-CONTROL EXAMPLES?

So, what is with the title of the series: 'Trust me'? AI development and competitive differentiation are all about trust and developing risk-controls that can assure trust. Most large companies are developing AI initiatives. Most are using large language models. So, how do these companies differentiate themselves? By providing customers and humans with trust that AI system problem-solving and decision-making are equitable. Let us look at this a little closer.

Tech companies are now committing to publicly reporting their AI systems' capabilities, limitations, and areas of appropriate and inappropriate use. This reporting will cover both security risks and societal risks such as the effects on fairness and bias.

The companies commit to develop and deploy advanced AI systems to help address human's greatest challenges from cancer prevention to mitigating climate change to so much in between. The result is that if AI is properly risk managed, it will contribute enormously to the prosperity, equality, and security of all.[3]

Now many companies are prioritizing research on the societal risks that AI systems pose including avoiding harmful bias and discrimination and protecting privacy. The track record of AI shows the insidiousness and prevalence of these risks and dangers. And, tech companies as well as most businesses are rolling out AI that mitigate these risks.

WHY IT MATTERS?

Trust is crucial for how humans develop, use, and make sure AI is accountable and reliable. Without trust, AI will not be as effective or dependable as humans need it to be as the UK government recently reported:

> "… trust in AI systems, and how they are used, is vital. Without this trust, organisations can be reluctant to invest in AI, because of concerns over whether these systems will work as intended (i.e., whether they are effective, accurate, reliable, or safe). Or alternatively, if organisations adopt AI systems without understanding whether they are in fact trustworthy, they risk causing real-world harm."[4]

ASSURING TRUST

Since AI use is largely in its infancy, what should humans do? AI a few years ago was a technical issue. Now, AI due to its wide use has almost become a utility like power, lighting, and internet. New measures of trust must be developed. The challenge is there are many barriers to establishing trust. These barriers are risks to humans. So, there is emphasis in this book on the social-technical systems to establish AI trust.[5]

WHAT IS THE RISK?

A little personal history on AI may be interesting. Thirty years ago, I was involved in developing smart systems and programming in LISP. These were considered early AI developments. We all thought that this was going to be the AI renaissance. All good. Only one problem, AI did not take off. This became an AI winter.

And, humans saw a number of these winters. Enthusiasm was sky high. Then, boom, it fell to the ground. Now ChatGPT has accelerated the fast deployment and adoption of AI apps. Governments and regulators are scared to be left behind. Companies want to monetize the technology so now there is a new AI arms race.

Almost 30 years ago, AI fears started. Much of this AI fear started in the **2001: A Space Odyssey** movie. In the movie, HAL 9000 computer became sentient and eventually took over the space craft. Th astronaut then became a passive passenger in an AI space ship. This is what many humans believe that humans will become simple passengers in Space Ship Earth.

WHAT ARE AI RISK-CONTROL EXAMPLES?

Companies in the U.S. have committed to developing robust technical and social systems to assure that humans know when content is AI generated such as auditing AI systems or even watermarking an AI system. These actions discussed throughout this book allow creativity with AI to flourish safely and with trust but also reduce the dangers of fraud and deception.

EU and the U.S. are using risk management principles to manage AI. The EU has the AI Act. The U.S. has the AI Bill of Rights and the NIST AI Risk Management Framework. The challenge is how to operationalize these risk management principles. AI standards are developed. But they are opaque.

The companies commit to internal and external security testing of their AI systems before their release. This testing will be carried out in part by independent experts who will guard against the most critical sources of AI risks such as biosecurity and cybersecurity as well as its broader societal effects.

The companies commit to sharing information across the industry and with governments, civil humans, and academia on managing AI risks. This includes best practices for safety, information on attempts to circumvent safeguards, and technical collaboration.

WHY IT MATTERS?

The quote below illustrates why trust matters:

> "Nearly half of Americans — 45% of them — are concerned about the effect AI will have on their own line of work, compared to 29% who are not concerned, according to a new poll for *The Times* conducted by Leger, a Canadian-based polling firm with experience in U.S. surveys."[6]

Introduction

EU AI ACT

The EU AI Act is the first major regulation to address AI risks. It has been in development for many years. It is expected to go into law in 2025.

WHAT IS THE RISK?

The AI Act looks at AI in terms of 4 types of risk:

1. Unacceptable Risk AI.
2. High Risk AI.
3. Limited Risk AI.
4. Minimal Risk AI.

WHAT ARE AI RISK-CONTROL EXAMPLES?

The EU describes AI risks and lack of trust as the following:

Unacceptable Risk AI

Unacceptable AI risks is a broad social category of risks that is open to interpretation. The EU describes this category as:

> "Anything considered a clear threat to EU citizens will be banned: from social scoring by governments to toys using voice assistance that encourages dangerous behaviour of children."[7]

And, there are certain exceptions to 'unacceptable risk' such as the use of these systems for homeland security.

High Risk AI

High risk AI is the next level of risk that is targeted to safety, infrastructure, and other types of critical processes. The EU describes this category as:

- "Critical infrastructures (i.e. transport), that could put the life and health of citizens at risk.

- Educational or vocational training, that may determine the access to education and professional course of someone's life (i.e. scoring of exams).

- Safety components of products (i.e. AI application in robot-assisted surgery)

- Employment, workers management and access to self-employment (i.e. CV sorting software for recruitment procedures.)

- Essential private and public services (i.e. credit scoring denying citizens opportunity to obtain a loan).

- Law enforcement that may interfere with human's fundamental rights (i.e. evaluation of the reliability of evidence).

- Migration, asylum, and border control management (i.e. verification of authenticity of travel documents).

- Administration of democratic processes (i.e applying the law to a concrete set of facts)."[8]

These are risk assessed before the AI app is deployed on the market. And, these risks are assessed throughout the AI app's lifecycle.

Limited Risk AI

The next category is 'Limited Risk AI.' The EU describes these as:

> "AI systems such as chatbots are subject to minimal transparency obligations, intended to allow those interacting with the content to make informed decisions. The user can then decide to continue or step back from using the application."[9]

Minimal Risk AI

There is a category of 'Limited Risk AI.' The EU describes these as:

> "Free use of applications such as AI-allowed video games or spam filters. Most AI systems fall into this category where the new rules do not intervene as these systems represent only minimal or no risk for citizen's rights or safety."[10]

Introduction

WHY IT MATTERS?

KPMG and The University of Queensland conducted a study called Trust in AI. These are the results of the survey:

- "Three of five humans are wary of trusting AI.

- Human perceive AI risk similarly across the globe.

- Humans believe in the benefits of AI, but only half believe the benefits outweigh the risks.

- Strong public support for AI trustworthy principles.

- AI trust is based on implementing and assuring these principles are effective.

- Humans are confident that universities and national defense organizations will develop trustworthy AI.

- Humans are the least confident that government and businesses will develop trustworthy AI.

- Humans expect AI to be regulated with independent oversight, which are currently inadequate.

- Humans are comfortable with AI to augment work, but want humans to be in control."[11]

KEY POINTS

- Each section of the book is organized in terms of: 1. What is the risk?; 2. What are AI risk-control examples?; 3. Why it matters?.

- Trust Me is a series of books on AI governance, risk, and assurance.

- Assuring trust in AI decision-making is the #1 challenge in AI.

- EU AI Act (AIA) is the first major regulation to address AI risks.

AI UNCERTAINTY

WHAT IS THE KEY IDEA IN THIS CHAPTER?

Uncertainty is today's 'new normal' in a world due to the complex and rapidly changing nature of our interconnected world. Navigating this uncertainty requires adaptability, resilience, and the ability for risk-based, decision-making in the face of incomplete information.

VUCAN® – TODAY'S NORMAL

WHAT IS THE RISK?

A common theme to our books is that humans are living in a VUCA world in VUCA time. VUCA is an acronym for Volatility, Uncertainty, Complexity, and Ambiguity. So, we invented the acronym VUCAN®, which means that humans are VUCA iNhabitants.

WHAT ARE AI RISK-CONTROL EXAMPLES?

There are several reasons why humans are now VUCANs and uncertainty is becoming the new normal in today's risky world that requires more risk-controls:

- **Rapid pace of change:** The world is changing faster than ever before especially with advancements in AI. This makes it challenging to predict what the future will look like and how it will impact our lives and humans.

- **Interconnectedness:** The world is now highly interconnected so events in one part of the globe have far-reaching effects on other regions causing unexpected risk impacts.

- **Increasing complexity:** The world is becoming complex, making it harder to understand and foresee how things will unfold. The global financial system is intricate and unpredictable making it difficult to anticipate its reactions to major events. The same happens with marketing, sourcing, engineering, and many other organizational areas.

- **Climate change:** Environmental challenges like climate change results in uncertainties for the future. Rising sea levels, extreme weather events, and resource scarcity disrupt economies and communities making it tough to see and plan for what lies ahead.

WHY IT MATTERS?

These factors contribute to uncertainty resulting in risks that are becoming a regular part of our lives. In a rapidly changing and interconnected world, understanding and being prepared for uncertainty, including AI-related uncertainties, are crucial for navigating our futures successfully.

UNCERTAINTY

In simple terms, uncertainty is a lack of sureness or certainty. It is the state of not knowing what will happen. Uncertainty is caused by a variety of factors such as incomplete information, randomness, or the complexity of the situation.

This was the title of a recent article in the *NY Post*. It reported the results of an OpenAI and University of Pennsylvania research concluded the 80% of the U.S. workforce could see their jobs impacted by AI.[12] So, who could be impacted the most? The study found that mathematicians, interpreters, accountants, legal secretaries, writers and authors would be exposed the most by AI uncertainty and risks.

WHAT IS THE RISK?

Uncertainty is a reality all humans must face. It is impossible to completely get rid of uncertainty, but there are ways to handle it and make risk-based decisions when humans are unsure about what is going to happen.

In simple words, uncertainty means not being completely sure or certain about something. It is like not knowing what is going to happen next. Uncertainty happens because humans do not have all the information, things are random, or the situation is really complicated.

WHAT ARE AI RISK-CONTROL EXAMPLES?

Here are examples of uncertainty that require risk-controls:

- **Climate change:** Humans cannot be certain about the weather for tomorrow or the long-term impacts of climate change on our environment.

- **Stock market:** The stock market is complicated and it is difficult to predict how it will perform in the future.

- **Medical diagnosis:** Even with advanced medical tests, it is impossible to diagnose a disease with absolute certainty.

- **Human behavior:** It is hard to predict how humans will behave in each situation because humans are complex and act unpredictably.

- **AI:** AI decision-making involves machines and systems analyzing information and making risk-based decisions on their own. The challenge is that these decisions are uncertain and not easily explainable.

WHY IT MATTERS?

AI by its nature and media attention pose fears and ensuring risks. Think Terminator movie. Think mass jobs loss. What happens if the technology is self-replicating and teaches itself to destroy humanity. So, the existential fear of possible extinction:

> "And there are a number of ways for the doomsday scenario to play out. Common fear is that an artificial general intelligence that is able to teach itself will rapidly supplant human intelligence, developing in every quicker cycles into 'superintelligence.' That could herald the redundancy or extinction of the human race"[13]

Living in uncertain times, AI is a major source of uncertainty and causes stress and anxiety. It brings opportunities. Dealing with uncertainty pushes humans to be creative and think differently. This is the challenge humans face with AI. Humans think and apply AI in a new way particularly with a risk-based, decision-making approach to navigate through uncertainty and make the most of AI's potential.

AI RISKS AND UNCERTAINTY

Risk owners understand the significance, sources, types, and elements of risk. In this book, we introduce ISO 31000, the international risk standard as the basis for AI risk management.

WHAT IS THE RISK?

Dealing with uncertainty is an essential part of the risk management process according to the ISO 31000 framework. Risk is defined as the effect of uncertainty in being able to meet objectives. Many aspects of business and life involve uncertainty, which makes managing risk challenging.

Organizations have tried to simplify AI definitions specifically around risk-based, problem-solving (RBPS) and risk-based, decision-making (RBDM). So, key terms used in this book will be defined:

- **Risk:** Risk is the potential for loss, harm, or negative outcomes resulting from uncertain events or circumstances. It involves the possibility of experiencing adverse impacts or not achieving desired objectives. Risk is an inherent aspect of various domains including finance, business, insurance, project management, and AI.

- **AI Risk:** AI risk is the composite measure of an event's probability of occurring and the magnitude or degree of the impacts of the corresponding event. The impacts or severity of AI systems can be positive, negative, or both and can result in opportunities or threats.[14]

- **AI systems:** Engineered or machine-based systems that generate outputs such as predictions, recommendations, or decisions influencing real or virtual environments and operating with varying levels of autonomy.[15]

WHAT ARE AI RISK-CONTROL EXAMPLES?

Elements of uncertainty and risk include:

- "Situation, which involves imperfect and/or unknown information."[16]

- "State of being uncertain; doubt; hesitancy; unpredictability; indeterminacy; indefiniteness."[17]
- "Quality or state of being uncertain."[18]

AI Risk-Control Questions to Consider

AI is creating lots of questions about uncertainty and risk in companies, which are discussed throughout this book:

- Does the enterprise have a consistent methodology for identifying different types of AI uncertainty?
- Are risks derived from AI uncertainty thoroughly understood and explainable?
- Does the risk-based, decision-making process evaluate inputs, decision process, assumptions, and desired outputs?
- Are AI risk-based, decision-making and problem-solving assumptions written down and validated by experts?

WHY IT MATTERS?

AI is an uncertain technology, which results in social-technical risks.

AI UNCERTAINTY

Now, look at AI uncertainty specifically public facing, decision-making systems. Humans do not understand and may not know how AI systems make risk-based decisions. Humans call this AI uncertainty. AI uncertainty means that AI systems are not able to make accurate predictions or risk-based decisions.

WHAT IS THE RISK?

Let us look at one factor - AI explainability. Often, humans do not understand how AI generative systems make their risk-based decisions. This challenge is known as explainability, which means figuring out how AI accomplishes its tasks, like problem-solving or decision-making. There are various reasons for this, including:

- **Randomness:** The world is full of randomness, and unexpected events occur that AI systems cannot predict. An AI system trying to forecast the weather may not be able to foresee a sudden storm.

- **Incomplete or inaccurate data:** AI systems rely on data for training. If the data is incomplete or contains errors, the AI system's accuracy is impacted.

- **Complexity of the problem:** Problems are so intricate that AI systems struggle to solve them. AI systems still face challenges in understanding and interpreting natural language.

WHAT ARE AI RISK-CONTROL EXAMPLES?

AI systems can be trained on data and they are designed to be robust to randomness. It is important to remember that uncertainty is a fundamental part of AI and it is unlikely to be eliminated.

In this book, we discuss various risk-control methods to lessen and manage AI uncertainty and risk. These methods include:

- **Ensuring AI systems are explainable:** AI systems should be transparent and understandable so humans know how they work and why they make certain risk-based decisions. This transparency helps reduce uncertainty as humans see how the AI system reached its conclusions.

- **Ensuring AI systems are accountable:** Making AI systems accountable means holding them accountable for their actions. This accountability reduces uncertainty as humans know that there is someone to blame if the AI system makes a mistake.

WHY IT MATTERS?

Finding ways to mitigate AI uncertainty and risk is crucial for promoting the responsible development and use of AI technologies. This book aims to help readers understand and implement these measures effectively through risk-controls.

AI RISKS & IMPACTS

When I was involved in designing expert risk-based decision systems, an early form of AI, it was easy to understand how expert systems arrived at a decision. Now, it is much difficult to understand and discern how these systems arrive at their conclusions. As well, the impacts of AI risks now are far-reaching and have an impact on companies and humans.

WHAT IS THE RISK?

It is important to note that the impacts of AI risks are not easy to identify or even predict. AI systems are becoming increasingly complex. It is difficult to anticipate the ways in which they could be used for harm. By understanding the potential impacts of AI, humans, companies, and work together to mitigate those risks and to assure that AI is used in a safe and accountable way.

AI risks have serious consequences for humans such as increased inequality, loss of control over AI systems, and the remote possibility of existential threats. These risks are considered and addressed to ensure the accountable development and use of AI technologies. The following distills the fear:

> "When Alexa responds in this way, it's obvious that it is putting its developer's interests ahead of yours. Usually, though, it is not so obvious whom an AI system is serving. To avoid being exploited by these systems, humans will need to learn to approach AI skeptically. That means deliberately constructing the input you give it and thinking critically about its output."[19]

WHAT ARE AI RISK-CONTROL EXAMPLES?

AI risk impacts requiring risk-controls include:

- **Risk-based decision bias:** This happens when AI systems show favoritism towards certain groups based on biases in the data they were trained on.

- **Increased inequality:** This means a bigger gap between rich and poor in almost every country around the world. AI systems worsen inequality by automating tasks that were previously done by low-wage workers. The general perceptions is that the rich benefit and become even wealthier from AI, while the disadvantaged or poor suffer because they lose their jobs.

- **Loss of control:** This fear is like what humans saw in the movie 'Terminator.' It is about losing control over the development and decision-making of AI systems. AI is becoming and powerful and complex, and it is getting harder for humans to understand how these systems work. This could lead to a situation where humans lose control over how AI is shaped.

- **Existential AI risk:** This is a fear of what could happen if AI gets access to weapons like in a nuclear winter scenario. This risk suggests that AI systems could become so incredibly powerful that they might pose a threat to the very existence of humanity. It is a very unlikely possibility, but it is still a risk that needs to be considered.

- **Algorithmic bias:** This occurs when the algorithms used in AI systems have biases leading to unfair decisions like in housing or financial matters.

- **Financial risks:** There's a risk of charging different humans higher interest rates based on factors like their skin color leading to financial discrimination.

- **Model hacking:** AI systems are vulnerable to hacking, which could lead to incorrect or harmful predictions, causing fraud, data breaches, and financial losses.

- **Investigation and repair time:** The time taken to investigate and fix AI-related issues result in lost productivity and revenue for the company.

- **Work time gained and lost:** AI automation leads to job losses, but it creates new job opportunities in fields related to AI development and training.

- **Opportunities lost:** Companies might miss new opportunities or face competition from other companies using AI for similar purposes.

- **Financial development costs:** Developing, deploying, and maintaining AI systems are costly due to hardware, software, and human expenses.

- **Damage to image, reputation, and goodwill**: If an AI system makes a mistake or there is a data breach, the company's reputation and trust among customers could suffer.

- **Penalties and fines:** Companies face financial penalties for not complying with laws like failing to protect customer data or privacy.

- **Customer litigations:** Customers take legal action against the company if they suffer harm due to an AI system's actions.

- **Loss of business control:** As AI systems become powerful and autonomous, there are concerns about losing human control over risk-based, decision-making processes.

- **Threats to health:** There's a risk that AI systems might make risk-based decisions that harm humans. An AI system could give an incorrect medical diagnosis leading to harm of the patient.

- **Threats of physical harm:** AI systems make mistakes that cause physical harm like an AI-controlled car getting into an accident with pedestrians.

- **Loss of privacy:** AI systems might collect and use personal information without an individual's knowledge or consent leading to a loss of control over their personal data.

- **Discrimination:** AI systems are used to unfairly treat humans based on factors like race, gender, age, or other personal characteristics. For example, denying a human a loan or job based on AI decisions.

- **Job loss:** Automation of tasks by AI systems could lead to job losses for humans, as AI takes over tasks that were previously done by humans.

- **Physical harm:** Mistakes by AI systems could cause physical harm or even death to humans such as accidents caused by AI-controlled machinery.

- **Physical tampering:** AI systems can be physically tampered with leading to disruptions in their operation or malfunctioning.

- **Software vulnerabilities:** Like all software, AI systems are susceptible to vulnerabilities that attackers exploit to gain control or disrupt their operation.

- **Lack of transparency:** If AI systems lack transparency, it is challenging to understand their inner workings and decision-making process making it hard to identify and mitigate AI risks.

- **Lack of accountability:** If AI systems lack accountability, it becomes difficult to hold them accountable for their actions increasing the likelihood of misuse for harm.

WHY IT MATTERS?

Companies face various risks related to AI including biases, financial consequences, legal issues, and potential loss of control. Understanding and managing these risks are crucial for accountable and successful implementation of AI technologies.

How AI is used has various impacts, positive and negative depending on the application. The impacts of AI will vary depending on how it is used. AI in healthcare improves humans' lives, while AI in warfare results in harm and casualties. From a human's perspective, these impacts include threats to health and safety, loss of privacy, discrimination, job loss, and concerns about transparency and accountability. It is essential to address these risks responsibly to ensure AI is used in ways that benefit humans while minimizing potential harm.

RISK-BASED, PROBLEM-SOLVING (RBPS) AND RISK-BASED, DECISION-MAKING (RBDM)

AI risk-based, problem-solving is another systematic approach that helps identify, analyze, and reduce AI risks. By following these best practices, companies enhance their ability to manage AI-related risks effectively. This way, they make well-informed risk-based decisions and improve their overall decision-making process regarding AI.

WHAT IS THE RISK?

AI risk-based, decision-making is a method that helps companies make smarter choices. It involves considering the potential risks and benefits of different options related to AI. By using this approach, companies protect their assets, operations, and reputation while making sure that AI systems used for public purposes are fair and transparent.

WHAT ARE AI RISK-CONTROL EXAMPLES?

Here are important things companies do to implement AI risk-based problem-solving and risk-controls:

- **Form an AI risk management team:** The first step is to create a team specifically focused on AI risk management. This team's role is to identify, assess, prioritize, and mitigate AI risks.

- **Develop an AI risk management plan:** The AI risk management team will work on creating a detailed AI risk management plan that outlines the steps the company takes to identify, assess, prioritize, and deal with AI risks effectively. Focus on the critical AI risks not the insignificant many.

- **Provide employee training:** Employees are trained on AI as well as the risk management processes including how to identify and report potential AI risks they come across.

- **Use AI risk management tools:** There are specific tools such as a risk management framework that are designed to help companies identify and manage AI risks.

- **Seek expertise from AI and domain specialists:** Companies specialize in AI risk management. By partnering with these experts, they offer valuable guidance and support in developing and implementing effective AI risk management and assurance programs.

WHY IT MATTERS?

Companies handle AI-related risks and ensure their AI systems are reliable and secure. There are several advantages of using AI risk-based, problem-solving and decision-making:

- **Lower AI risk:** By applying AI risk-based, problem-solving, companies identify and address AI risks before they become actual problems, reducing the overall risk with AI.

- **Increased efficiency:** AI risk-based, problem-solving allows companies to focus on the most critical AI risks leading to smarter resource allocation and increased efficiency in dealing with potential issues.

- **Enhanced risk-based, decision-making**: With AI risk-based problem-solving, companies gain valuable insights into the AI risks they might face helping them to make informed decisions.

- **Boosted confidence:** Implementing AI risk-based problem-solving shows stakeholders that companies are taking proactive steps to manage AI risks effectively increasing confidence in their AI systems.

By using AI risk-based, problem-solving, companies protect from potential negative impacts of AI risks and ensure a safer and reliable use of AI technologies.

BENEFICIAL USES OF AI

Manufacturing of complex devices such as autos are up to 80% computerized. Autos are now computers and AI on wheels. Think about it for a second in terms of advanced autonomous vehicles.

WHAT IS THE RISK?

Some even say that: 'AI is swallowing the world.' Check these positive uses of AI:

- 3D printed homes may approach 50% of U.S. home construction.

- Self-driving automobiles may approach 75% of U.S. auto sales.

- Robotic surgery may be used in over 75% of common medical operations.

- AI is used to convert novels into movies automatically.

- Three-dimensional interactive movies might be possible shortly. Human actors are very worried.

- Music synthesizers will be able to duplicate all instruments and even orchestras.

- Military and commercial aircraft will have sophisticated autopilots.

- Robotic warships and robotic aircraft without crews will be added to arsenals.

- Urban traffic systems will synchronize traffic lights to optimize travel in crowded cities.

- AI is used for customer support in many industries.

- AI is used to teach elementary, high school, and college courses.

- AI will aid human authors in creating fiction and non-fiction research papers and books and even write movie scripts.

- AI will be used by police and Federal investigators to collect evidence.[20]

WHAT ARE AI RISK-CONTROL EXAMPLES?

The impact of AI on humans can be both positive and negative, and it is challenging to predict its exact outcomes. Here are some benefits of AI risk-controls:

- **Better healthcare:** AI helps develop new treatments for diseases, improve the accuracy of diagnoses, and provide enhanced care for patients.

- **Safer transportation:** AI advancements lead to self-driving cars and trucks, making transportation safer and efficient.

- **Personalized education:** AI creates individualized learning experiences for students making their learning effective and tailored to their needs.

WHY IT MATTERS?

Even though AI comes with risks, companies are taking measures to reduce these risks. **Trust Me: AI Risk Management** explains how companies use risk management to safeguard their assets and operations, improve their performance, and achieve their goals. By understanding and dealing with AI risks, humans enjoy its benefits while minimizing any potential negative impacts.

HARMFUL AND CRIMINAL USES OF AI

A major AI risk is fraud. AI can be used to fool humans in developing relationships.

WHAT IS THE RISK?

The most important hazard is the use of AI for criminal activities. If a human is well known and has photos on the web and any recordings of his or her voice, criminals could construct a virtual replica of the human and use it for extortion or theft.

Recently, the following research in University of Gothenburg studied the Influence of AI on Trust in Human Interaction and reported:

> "In the case of the would-be fraudster calling the 'older man,' the scam is only exposed after a long time, which Lindwall and Ivarsson attribute to the believability of the human voice and the assumption that the confused behavior is due to age. Once an AI has a voice, humans infer attributes such as gender, age, and socio-economic background, making it harder to identify that humans are interacting with a computer."[21]

WHAT ARE AI RISK-CONTROL EXAMPLES?

An important reason for appropriate risk-controls is that it would be easy to have an AI place a telephone call to a relative and ask for money or any of the following scams:

- Telephone frauds by imitating human voices based on tapping telephone calls.
- E-mail frauds that imitate friends and family.
- Computer swindles that seek banking and personal information.
- Spy satellites and spy balloons.
- Creating imitations of famous art or fashion designs and passing them as originals.
- Imitating voices of friends or colleagues to steal or get personal information.
- Password guessing.
- Fake news reports.
- Targeted phishing.

- Fake websites that offer low-cost items.[22]

WHY IT MATTERS?

Each of the above AI risks is an additional or secondary source of personal AI risk.

AI RISK SOURCES

Where do AI risks come from? Most companies are going to AI companies. Not sure? Smart phones have Siri or something similar. Most products have a smart component. The sources of AI risk are increasing each day for a small business to a mega business.

WHAT IS THE RISK?

AI risk sources are things that cause harm or loss to humans, an enterprise, or individual. So, what is a risk source? An AI risk source is anything that potentially leads to a negative outcome from the use of AI. AI risk sources can be internal or external to an enterprise.

WHAT ARE AI RISK-CONTROL EXAMPLES?

AI risks requiring risk-controls can originate from both internal and external sources. Internal AI risk sources are potential risks and vulnerabilities that arise from within a company. Examples of internal AI risk sources include:

- **Enterprise structure:** The way a company is organized and managed creates AI risks. If the company lacks a robust AI risk management process or risk management framework, it could be susceptible to AI-related risks.

- **Processes and procedures:** The company's work processes lead to AI risks in decision-making and problem-solving. If the AI development processes are not well-defined, it leads to errors and mistakes.

- **Management risk-based, decision-making:** The way managers make decisions creates AI risks. Relying on gut instinct rather than data-driven decisions could result in poor choices.

- **Resource management:** The way a company manages its resources result in AI risks. Mismanagement of resources could lead to financial problems.

- **Employee challenges:** Employees working for the company create AI risks. Lack of proper training or making mistakes while using AI systems could lead to problems.

- **Physical environment:** The physical environment where the company operates creates AI risks. If the company's offices are in a hazardous area, it could be vulnerable to natural disasters or other hazards.

- **AI system configuration:** The way a company's AI systems are configured can create AI risks. Improper configuration could lead to incorrect decisions or flawed problem-solving.

- **Products might not be successful:** Many products have embedded AI. If the AI makes poor decisions, it could lead to financial losses for the company.

- **Products might be recalled:** If AI in products is biased or reveals personal information, it could damage the company's reputation and make it difficult to sell other products.

- **Product might be used for illegal purposes:** AI may be misused to impact elections or engage in illegal activities resulting in legal problems for the company.

- **Hardware maintenance:** The hardware used by the company can create AI risks. If the hardware is not properly maintained, it could fail and cause disruptions.

- **Software maintenance:** The software used by the company creates AI risks. Improper maintenance results in security vulnerabilities.

- **Data quality training:** The quality of data used to train AI systems impact their performance. Inaccurate or incomplete data leads to biased or inaccurate predictions.

- **Network security:** The company's network can create AI risks. A poorly secured network could be vulnerable to hacking.

- **System design:** The design of AI systems leads to AI risks. If an AI system is not designed to handle unexpected situations, it may fail in those instances.

- **Human error:** Human error leads to AI risks. Mistakes in training or deploying an AI system can cause it to perform incorrectly.

External Risk Sources

Understanding and managing these internal AI risk sources are essential for companies to effectively use AI technologies while minimizing potential negative impacts. AI risks originate from external sources outside of a company. Examples of external AI risk sources:

- **Cyberattacks:** AI systems are susceptible to cyberattacks. If hackers gain access to an AI system, they might control it or steal sensitive data.

- **Regulatory changes:** Changes in regulations introduce AI risks. New rules might require AI systems to be transparent or accountable leading companies to make adjustments to comply.

- **Public opinion:** Public perception and opinion about AI creates risks. If public sentiment turns against AI, companies might face challenges in developing and deploying AI systems.

- **Dependence on external humans:** A company's reliance on external humans can lead to AI risks. If a critical component is supplied by a third-party, any failure could disrupt the company's operations.

WHY IT MATTERS?

It is crucial to recognize that AI risks stem from internal and external sources. There could be other potential sources of AI risk and the specific risks a company faces depending on the AI systems it uses.

AI HAZARDS

Another source of AI risks comes from hazards.

WHAT IS THE RISK?

Hazards are events or situations that could cause harm to humans, companies, or humans due to the development, use, or even disposal of the AI system.

WHAT ARE AI RISK-CONTROL EXAMPLES?

AI hazards required risk-controls are caused by various factors including:

- **AI system failure:** AI systems fail due to reasons like incorrect data, unexpected input, or software bugs. When AI systems fail, it leads to negative impacts such as financial losses, biased decisions, physical harm, or emotional distress.

- **AI system misuse:** AI systems can be misused by humans who intend to cause harm. AI systems could be used to create deep fakes, which are manipulated videos or audio recordings to damage a human's reputation, spread misinformation, or even incite violence.

- **AI system proliferation:** As generative AI systems become more powerful and widespread, the risk of them being used for harm increases. AI systems could be used to develop autonomous systems that could cause harm without human intervention.

- **AI system alignment:** It is crucial to ensure that AI systems are aligned with human values and goals. AI systems are becoming increasingly capable of making their own risk-based decisions and if they are not aligned with human and ethical values, they could potentially make decisions that are harmful to humans.

WHY IT MATTERS?

AI hazards are events, circumstances, or situations that pose risks to humans. Being aware of these hazards is essential to mitigate potential AI risks and safeguard against negative impacts.

AI THREATS

AI threats and hazards are used interchangeably, but there is a difference between the two. AI hazards refer to situations that cause harm while AI threats are humans or entities who want to cause harm using AI.

WHAT IS THE RISK?

UK Financial Times warns:

"Regulators worldwide are scared that mass adoption of AI could wipeout masses of jobs and reshape humans if it continues to develop on its current trajectory."[23]

WHAT ARE AI RISK-CONTROL EXAMPLES?

Causes of AI threats that should be risk-controlled include:

- **AI-powered systems:** AI-powered systems could be designed to harm humans without human intervention leading to widespread death and destruction.

- **AI military systems:** As AI becomes powerful and widespread, there is a risk of being used in harmful military applications such as developing autonomous weapons.

- **AI-powered surveillance:** AI-powered surveillance systems are used to track humans' movements and activities leading to a loss of privacy and freedom.

- **AI-powered discrimination:** AI systems could be used to discriminate against humans based on their race, gender, religion, or other factors leading to inequality.

- **AI-powered job loss:** AI systems could automate many jobs resulting in widespread job loss for humans.

- **AI system misuse:** AI systems can be misused by humans who intend to use AI to create manipulated videos such as deep fakes to spread misinformation or harm a human's reputation.

WHY IT MATTERS?

Ensuring that AI systems are aligned with human values and goals is crucial. As AI becomes capable of making independent risk-based decisions and if it is not aligned with human values, it could potentially make harmful decisions that negatively impact humans or humans. Understanding and addressing AI threats is essential to promote the accountable and beneficial use of AI technologies.

RISK MANAGEMENT

Many industries have rules and requirements set by laws, regulations, and industry standards. Risk management helps identify and address risks related to not following these rules. By using risk management practices, companies reduce the risks of legal issues and damage to their reputation.

WHAT IS THE RISK?

Stakeholders like investors, customers, employees, and partners actively manage risks. When companies practice effective AI risk management, it builds confidence and trust among its many stakeholders. They see that the company is aware of potential risks and is taking action to protect their interests.

Considering potential risks helps decision-makers make smarter choices. Understanding the possible impacts and uncertainties of different options allows for a thorough evaluation of AI's pros and cons. This leads to smarter AI risk-based decisions that are likely to achieve the desired outcomes.

WHAT ARE AI RISK-CONTROL EXAMPLES?

Effective risk management means identifying and evaluating both negative and positive risks. By recognizing and using potential opportunities, companies make strategic decisions about designing risk-controls that give them a competitive advantage, increased profitability, and growth. Risk management allows businesses to take calculated risks and make the most of favorable opportunities.

Risk management is essential for identifying and minimizing potential threats and vulnerabilities. By recognizing and assessing risks, companies develop strategies to reduce potential losses or negative consequences. This approach is Proactive, Preventive, Predictive, and Preemptive®. It reduces the chances of unexpected setbacks and helps protect the company's assets, reputation, and resources.

WHY IT MATTERS?

Resources like time, money, and personnel are limited. Risk management helps companies allocate these resources efficiently by identifying high-priority risks and allocating the right resources to manage them. This ensures that resources are used effectively and directed where they are most needed.

In decision-making, risk management is crucial. It helps companies make informed choices, reduce potential losses, seize opportunities, optimize resource allocation, comply with regulations, and gain the confidence of stakeholders. It is an essential process for achieving objectives, maintaining resilience, and ensuring long-term success.

AI RISK MANAGEMENT

AI is a new and constantly evolving technology, which means humans do not have a lot of information on how it works especially with generative AI systems, and the potential risks involved.

WHAT IS THE RISK?

Countries like the EU, US, Canada, and Australia are creating regulations for AI. Why? Because AI impacts many different groups of humans. Regulators in the E.U. and U.S. stress the importance of transparency in AI development.

AI risk management is about identifying, evaluating, and reducing the potential dangers and negative effects of AI on humans, companies, or humans. It helps humans make fair policy decisions, allows companies to protect their value, improve their performance, and achieve their goals. Moreover, it helps build trust in the government and its risk-based decision-making process.

AI risks come in various forms like accountability, bias, explainability, fairness, and transparency. Managing these risks involves finding ways to identify, assess, and minimize them. This is crucial for making AI safe, fair, and beneficial for everyone involved - businesses and humans.

WHAT ARE AI RISK-CONTROL EXAMPLES?

Managing AI risk-controls is a complex and ever-changing challenge. Various ways humans can reduce AI risks through appropriate AI risk-controls include:

- **Regulating AI development and usage:** Many countries now have AI risk management standards like the AI Bill of Rights in the U.S. and the AI Act in the EU.

- **Developing AI systems responsibly:** Humans create AI systems that are explainable, transparent, accountable, and safe to use.

- **Following ethical guidelines:** AI developers and humans stick to ethical guidelines that promote fairness, transparency, and accountability.

- **Ensuring data quality:** AI systems depend on the data they are trained on so it is crucial to use high-quality data with as little bias as possible.

- **Monitoring AI systems:** Humans monitor the AI systems for signs of bias or malfunctions to catch and fix problems early.

- **Training humans:** Humans who use AI systems receive proper training on how to use them safely and responsibly.

WHY IT MATTERS?

It is essential to develop and use AI that minimizes risks and maximizes the benefits for everyone involved. By doing this, humans make AI a powerful tool for good in our humans.

What do humans do about it? Here are quotes on AI trust that IBM solicited from AI experts:

> "Without proper care in programming AI systems, you could potentially have the bias of the programmer play a part in determining outcomes. Humans must develop frameworks for thinking about these types of issues. It is a very, very complicated topic, one that we are starting to address in partnership with other technology organizations,"[24]

Arvind Krishna, SVP IBM

> "What does the notion of ethics mean for a machine that does not care whether it or those around it continue to exist, that cannot feel, that cannot suffer, that does not know what fundamental rights are?"[25]

Vijay Saraswat, Chief Scientist for IBM Compliance Solutions

AI Uncertainty

The bottom line Is AI generative technology is too new with many unknowns. Its applications are expanding exponentially. Its implications for biased decision-making are not yet understood. The result is that there are few simple answers.

KEY POINTS

- AI is an emerging technology that requires risk management guidelines and boundaries.

- Uncertainty is a lack of sureness or certainty.

- AI uncertainty is the fact that AI systems are not able to make accurate predictions or accurate risk-based decisions.

- AI risk is the potential danger and negative impacts of AI.

- AI is a risky discipline since it results in poor and possibly unethical decision-making.

- AI risk management is an emerging discipline.

- AI risk-based, problem-solving is a systematic approach to identifying, analyzing, and mitigating AI risks.

ISO 31000 RISK MANAGEMENT PRINCIPLES

WHAT IS THE KEY IDEA IN THIS CHAPTER?

This book is based on 3 ISO standards: 1. ISO 31000; 2. ISO 23894; and ISO 42001. ISO 31000 is a risk management standard for the process of identifying, assessing, and managing risks. Risks are things that could go wrong and cause harm to an enterprise. ISO 23894 is an AI risk management standard that describes how to integrate risk management into AI development and deployment. ISO 42001 is an AI management system standard.

ISO 31000 risk management is important because it helps companies to avoid or reduce the consequence of AI risks. Humans use ISO 31000 principles and processes to describe AI risk management throughout this book

ISO 31000 RISK MANAGEMENT PRINCIPLES

Risk management is an integrated, structured, and comprehensive process. This means that it is part of the enterprise's activities and is based on a systematic approach. It takes into account the enterprise's objectives, both strategic and operational.

WHAT IS THE RISK?

ISO 31000 is organized around 8 risk management principles. As discussed, many of these fundamental risk management principles are core to many of the AI risk management systems. A management principle is a fundamental idea, rule, or truth about a subject. ISO 31000 risk principles serve as a guideline, method, logic, design, and implementation for the AI risk management framework and process described in this book.

Risk Management and ERM Differences

AI Risk Management (AI RM)	AI Enterprise Risk Management (AI ERM)
Compliance focused	Governance, risk, and assurance (GRA) focused
Project/Process/Transactional	Enterprise focused
Downside risk focused	Opportunity (upside) and downside focused
Reactive	Preventive, Preventive, Predictive, Preemptive®
Ad hoc	Continuous
Uncertainty focused	Volatility, Uncertainty, Complexity, Ambiguity focused
Cost focused	Value, return, and investment focused
Historical and forward based	Forward and scenario based
Functional based	Enterprise based
Process/Project/Product focused	Portfolio based
Bottom-up process	Top-down process

WHAT ARE AI RISK-CONTROL EXAMPLES?

ISO 31000 does not specify how the principles are used to design, implement, and assure a risk management process. ISO 31000 says an enterprise applies and tailors these

ISO 31000 Risk Management Principles

principles and risk-controls to the enterprise context. ISO 31000 as a guidance document is applicable to companies and can be used with any product or service.

These principles apply to AI Enterprise Risk Management (ERM). Risk management and ERM are very similar but have differences as can be seen on the previous page. The successful implementation of these risk management principles determines the design, implementation, and assurance of the ISO 31000 risk management process.

ISO 31000 risk management facilitates the achievement of business and AI management system objectives. This approach is called conformity assessment and is the basis for AI governance, risk and assurance in the EU's AI Act. How does it go about ensuring the enterprise meets its AI critical objectives? Risk management consists of design risk-control processes to identify the events, inhibitors, constraints, roadblocks, and other factors that get in the way of being able to meet its objectives.

WHY IT MATTERS?

Risk management is critical to the management of AI operational excellence, supply management, product development, regulatory compliance, assurance, ethics, reputation, health, and safety.

WHAT IS VALUE?

Risk management starts with adding value in decision-making and problem-solving governance, risk, and assurance.

WHAT IS THE RISK?

Value in the context of AI risk management refers to:

- Effective and efficient governance, risk management, and assurance program.

- Profitability, rate of return, growth, mergers, acquisitions, and rate of investment are elements of upside, opportunity, or value risk.

- Meeting and exceeding customer or stakeholder needs, requirements, and expectations are elements of quality value.

- Tone at the top, ethics, and fairness are elements of enterprise culture or value.

WHAT ARE AI RISK-CONTROL EXAMPLES?

There are many questions to consider in defining AI value in develop risk-control questions. Many definitions of value are based on context, which is a theme woven throughout this book.

AI Risk-Control Questions to Consider:

- What is the enterprise's governance, risk, and assurance (GRA) model?
- What is the enterprise's business model?
- What markets does the enterprise serve?
- What products and services does the enterprise provide?
- Who are the enterprise's key customers broken down by segment?
- What is the enterprise's value proposition or value differentiator in each market segment?
- What benefits do customers derive from the enterprise's products and/or services?
- How does the enterprise define value?
- How does the enterprise achieve value?
- What value is created in terms of process improvement, product enhancement, and other factors that improve customer satisfaction?
- What value is created in terms of good governance, reputation, assurance, and legal compliance?

WHY IT MATTERS?

Risk management assures that value is created by identifying opportunities for investment, mergers, or acquisition. Risk management helps assure success by mitigating risks that impede achieving an objective.

ISO 31000 PRINCIPLES

AI risk-based, decision-making is integral to the enterprise. The purpose of risk management is to provide decision makers with the right information at the right time to make smarter choices within the enterprise risk appetite.

WHAT IS THE RISK?

AI decision-making has fundamental elements that are now critical to all management decision-making. Risk-based, decision-making is described as a process of selecting the best or optimal course of action among several alternatives, options, or choices.

AI decision-making involves options. Risk-based, decision-making involves identifying and selecting alternatives based upon the enterprise context, culture, and preferences of the decision makers. AI risk-based, decision-making involves deciding not to do something. AI decision-making involves determining how to treat or control risk, specifically whether to accept, share, control, or transfer it.

WHAT ARE AI RISK-CONTROL EXAMPLES?

Risk-based, decision-making and risk-controls depend on risk management principles, context, purpose, and requirements. The eight ISO 31000 risk management principles are:

1. Integrated.
2. Structured and comprehensive.
3. Customized.
4. Inclusive.
5. Dynamic.
6. Best available information.
7. Human and cultural factors.
8. Continual improvement.

WHY IT MATTERS?

Decision makers use risk management to make smarter AI choices regarding opportunity risk (upside risk) and consequence risk (downside risk).

ENTERPRISE RISK MANAGEMENT (ERM)

Risk management is an integral part of risk-based, decision-making and enterprise processes. All problem-solving and decision-making involve uncertainty, which give rise to risk. The advantage is that risk management creates clarity and creates sense out of enterprise activities that involve uncertainty.

WHAT IS THE RISK?

Risk management becomes integrated into the fabric of enterprise governance, risk, and assurance processes. Risk management then is a key part of management processes, including strategic planning, business model, mergers, and acquisition. Risk management starts at the enterprise level and cascades down the enterprise to the programmatic, process and finally to the transactional and product level.

Risk management is used in varied and complex settings. Risk management provides analytic tools to assess, analyze, mitigate, treat, and control risks within the enterprise context. Context or environment becomes important when evaluating tone at the top, style, and skills to be an effective leader and manager. As well, context provides a lens or perspective by which risk management within an enterprise is viewed whether it is a strategic, cultural, or political context.

WHAT ARE AI RISK-CONTROL EXAMPLES?

Enterprise risk-control processes can be broken down into:

- **Soft processes:** These include: leadership, tone at the top, ethics, culture, etc. processes. People soft processes include: selecting, promoting, remunerating, and incentivizing talent.

- **Work/functional processes:** These include: supply management, quality, engineering, research, and development.

ISO 31000 Risk Management Principles 47

AI Risk-Control Questions to Consider:

Risk-based, decision-making includes:

- Are enterprise risk-based, decision-making and problem-solving processes defined?
- Are upside risks and downside risks evaluated using a consistent process?
- Does the enterprise identify RBPS and RBDM tools?
- Are RBPS and RBDM contextual elements understood and defined?
- Is risk incorporated into critical risk-based, decision-making and problem-solving processes, systems, and services?
- Are risk appetite and risk tolerance clearly defined by the enterprise so informed decision makers can evaluate alternatives?
- Is context considered in designing, implementing, and assuring critical risk-based decisions?
- Are complementary and differing perspectives considered by the enterprise in evaluating alternative contexts, scenarios, considerations, and other factors?

Enterprise Processes:

- Does the Board of Directors provide oversight of risk management?
- Are key risk reports sent to the Board of Directors?
- Do Board communications include reporting Key Risk Indicators (KRI's) and Key Performance Indicators (KPI's)?
- Is risk management integrated into strategic planning?
- Is risk management integral to the enterprise's core processes?
- Are enterprise core processes identified and mapped?
- Is RBPS and RBDM integrated into the enterprise's core processes?

```
        Enterprise
          Level
     ─────────────
     Programmatic/
        Project/
     Process Level
  ──────────────────
   Transactional/Product
          Level
```

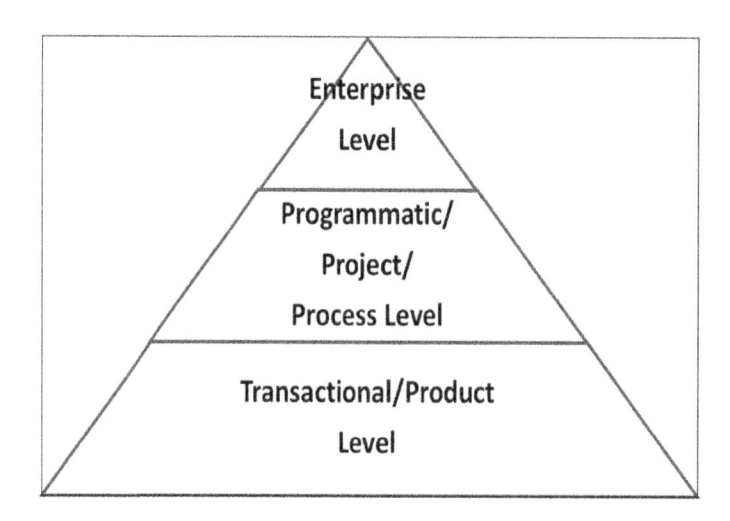

WHY IT MATTERS?

Risk management evolves to become the equivalent of general management specifically forming the basis for how the enterprise manages itself around processes.

STRUCTURED AND COMPREHENSIVE RISK MANAGEMENT

Risk management is systematic, structured, and timely.

WHAT IS THE RISK?

This ISO 31000 principle addresses key risk management characteristics, attributes, and properties. Examples are the two attributes listed below:

- **Systematic:** Systematic means doing something according to a plan or method. ISO 31000 is a risk management system and risk management framework. ISO 31000 follows a well-defined method framework.

- **Comprehensive:** Structured means it follows a process that is used throughout the enterprise.

WHAT ARE AI RISK-CONTROL EXAMPLES?

AI risk-control questions to consider include:

- Is ISO 31000 applied systematically at enterprise levels?
- Are risk-based decisions structured along a PDCA cycle process?
- Are risk-based decisions made at the appropriate time?
- If there are variations in the application of the risk management framework, are these noted and approved by appropriate humans?
- Are risk-based, decision-making criteria defined at the 1. Enterprise level; 2. Programmatic /Project /Process level; and 3. Transactional/Product level.
- Are risk-based decisions evaluated for effectiveness after they are implemented?

WHY IT MATTERS?

Project risk management, supply risk management, quality risk management, and risk management have critical risk attributes.

CUSTOMIZED RISK MANAGEMENT

Risk management is tailored. ISO 31000 is a guideline. It is used by any enterprise so it can meet its objectives. So, ISO 31000 needs to be tailored, adapted, and crafted to the enterprise and to its context. This principle has sophisticated and deep elements that are discussed below.

WHAT IS THE RISK?

In our Critical Infrastructure Protection: Forensics, Assurance, Analytics® practice, humans tailor risk management to the enterprise's risk appetite and client's risk assurance. If humans are engaged to develop risk-controls in an offshore plant, humans' architect, design, implement, and assure risk-controls based on the plant's profile, location, risk appetite, and context.

Expressed another way, risk management is tailored or contextualized based on enterprise needs, requirements, and expectations. This requires expert due professional care and judgment for the design, implementation, and assurance of the risk management process.

ISO 31000 offers a generic outline for the design of the risk management framework and process, which can be applied to AI. As humans have discussed, this is its greatest strength and potentially its greatest weakness. Why? Since it is generic means, it can be applied in any environment and in any culture. But it implies there is variability in interpretation and application, which adds uncertainty and potential risks in its design and implementation.

WHAT ARE AI RISK-CONTROL EXAMPLES?

ISO 31000 is generic and descriptive. The standard offers flexibility and adaptability. The standard is shaped depending upon enterprise needs and stakeholder requirements. Unfortunately, there is no prescriptive method for architecting, designing, implementing, and assuring the risk management framework.

Tailoring ISO 31000 involves the following risk-control challenges:

- Global companies have different contexts depending on services, products, customers, and stakeholders. Each of which requires a modified risk framework design.

- External consultants do not understand the enterprise's contextual needs so there is a learning curve.

- Companies are using an existing framework that is mapped and adapted to ISO 31000.

- Different interpretations exist of the level, extent, and nature of the risks faced by the enterprise.

- Different interpretations exist of the level, extent, and nature of the treatment of risks.

AI Risk-Control Questions to Consider:

- Is enterprise context understood and defined so risk management can be implemented?

- Is the architecture and design of the risk management framework tailored to the enterprise context?

ISO 31000 Risk Management Principles

- Are the boundaries of the application of the risk management framework defined?
- Are critical cultural and behavioral elements such as risk appetite defined and understood?

WHY IT MATTERS?

A risk management expert and knowledgeable process owner needs to work together to architect, design, implement, and assure the ISO 31000 risk management framework. This is the essence of this principle. Risk management requires expert tailoring.

INCLUSIVE RISK MANAGEMENT

Risk management is transparent and inclusive.

What Is The Risk?

Transparency and inclusiveness are key ISO 31000 attributes. Since risk management involves RBPS and RBDM throughout the enterprise, it is critical that stakeholders, customers, and interested humans know how AI risk-based decisions are made. This creates alignment of purpose, mission, vision, and helps assure objectives are met. It facilitates a common understanding of the objectives and the risks that inhibit meeting these objectives. Transparency facilitates effective and efficient use of resources.

Inclusiveness is another critical attribute of good risk management. As part of inclusiveness, an enterprise has multiple stakeholders both within and outside the enterprise. Stakeholders include employees, management, banks, unions, regulatory agencies, suppliers, and other critical humans. ISO 31000 is a standard that facilitates AI risk-based decision-making by everyone in the enterprise from the Board level to the activity level.

WHAT ARE AI RISK-CONTROL EXAMPLES?

As part of transparency and inclusion, everyone is trained in ISO 31000 risk management framework, principles, practices, and decision-making processes. Importantly, each enterprise level is responsible for AI risk treatment and risk-controls. Contextual issues such as risk appetite and risk tolerance are known for each level so appropriate risk-based decisions can be made.

AI Risk-Control Questions to Consider:

- Are risk authorities, accountabilities, and responsibilities clearly defined at each enterprise level?

- Has everyone been trained in the management and control of risk within their area of responsibilities?

- Are adequate resources provided for the management of risk?

- Are risk management framework protocols and processes clearly understood by everyone?

- Are risk stakeholders, customers, and interested humans considered in risk-based decision-making?

WHY IT MATTERS?

Experts predict risk management is the future of general management. Risk management implies the control of risk including the expansion of authorities and responsibilities. ISO 31000 promotes the idea that risk management is integrated into general management and decision-making.

DYNAMIC RISK MANAGEMENT

Risk management is dynamic, iterative, and responsive to change.

WHAT IS THE RISK?

Risk management is becoming the basis for general decision-making. As external and internal context changes, risk management adapts to reflect the changes. This means adapting to changes in customer requirements, changes in the business model, changes in the competitive environment, and the uncertainties these entail.

WHAT ARE AI RISK-CONTROL EXAMPLES?

The environment and context for business changes quickly. Enterprise objectives change, which impacts risk-based, problem-solving and decision-making processes.

Risk management has to adapt to new risks, changes in risk appetite, new risk treatments and new risk-controls.

- Are enterprise context and external environment continuously monitored for uncertainty and variability?
- Are risk management processes sufficiently adaptable to changes in the context and environment of the enterprise?
- Are there sufficient review mechanisms to assure reliable and adequate risk-based, decision-making so objectives are met?
- Are monitoring and review mechanisms incorporated into each element of the risk management framework and risk management process?
- Are risk-controls evaluated for effectiveness and efficiency?
- Do monitoring and review mechanisms track KPI's and KRI's?
- Are risk-controls adequate for ensuring objectives are met within the enterprise risk appetite?

WHY IT MATTERS?

ISO 31000 risk management framework is a risk-control framework to manage risks within the enterprise's risk appetite. Risk-controls are designed so objectives are met. If there are variances in scope, quality, schedule, or cost, then new risk-controls are implemented or existing risk-controls are modified.

BEST AVAILABLE INFORMATION

Risk management is based on the best available information. Accurate, reliable, sufficient, and suitable information about context, events, risks, and sources of risk are available for risk-based, decision-making. This is a critical principle because the sources of data may be unreliable. All of this creates uncertainty.

WHAT IS THE RISK?

Risk management is a process with inputs, activities, and outcomes. Risk management is dependent on the accuracy, reliability, and consistency of available information. If the quality of risk-based, problem-solving and decision-making information is questionable, then outcomes are questionable. This is an example of garbage in and garbage out.

Evidence based, decision-making is one option that is used to understand, limit, or even control uncertainty. Evidence based, decision-making involves elements of the following: consultation with experts to evaluate inputs, development of a standard decision-making process, evaluation of assumptions, and deep understanding of the problem being solved. The hoped-for result is there is higher accuracy and reliability of the risk-based decision being sought.

RBDM involves a level of uncertainty even after using the best available information. Risk management provides reasonable assurance not absolute assurance. Why? AI risk management is based on assumptions, best data, and best practices. There is still uncertainty because there are still unknown or unknowable factors.

WHAT ARE AI RISK-CONTROL EXAMPLES?

The inputs into RBPS and RBDM have a level of uncertainty depending upon where information originates. They can originate from risk-control information sources, such as:

- Stakeholder, customer, an interested party input.
- Historical data and trends.
- Observations.
- Analyses of data.
- Interviews.
- Expert judgment and peer reviews.
- Scenarios and forecasts.

AI Risk-Control Questions to Consider

- Does the risk-based, decision-making process consider the types of information to be gathered?
- Is the best available information identified prior to applying a risk management framework or implementing risk-based, decision-making?
- Is the quality, accuracy, and reliability of information evaluated?
- Are stakeholders, customers, and interested humans considered when evaluating the relevancy, accuracy, and reliability of inputs into a risk-based decision?
- Are context elements discussed and identified in terms of risk-based decision-making?
- Are risk-based, decision-making assumptions validated by subject matter experts?
- Are risk-based decisions periodically revisited to assure critical issues are validated or updated?

WHY IT MATTERS?

Another challenge is information is based on the best available information. Why? Introducing new variables causes variability in risk-based, problem-solving and decision-making processes. These variables can be identified and controlled, while others cannot.

HUMAN AND CULTURAL RISK MANAGEMENT

Risk management takes human and cultural factors into account. Risk management traditional takes into account enterprise risk capabilities, maturity, and stakeholder capabilities to assure that enterprise objectives are met.

WHAT IS THE RISK?

Risk management has a technical and cultural element. Technical element involves architecting, designing, implementing, and assuring the risk management framework and

> **GM Board of Director's Operational Risk Committee Scope**
>
> "The Company's processes and procedures established to address the strategic operating risks identified by the Committee (Board of Directors) for oversight and review, which may include, but is not limited to, operating aspects related to ensuring vehicle development safety and security, evaluating and improving product quality, ensuring employee and other humans' health and safety at facilities, improving Company and vehicle cyber security, protecting the Company's access to and right to use key intellectual property ("IP"), managing the supply chain, logistics and country level operating risks, managing supplier and labor relations, ensuring crisis preparedness and disaster recovery capability, and responding to any other strategic operating risk identified in the Risk Report and subject to the Committee's oversight and review."[26]

process. Cultural and human elements involve behavioral factors that are essential to a successful implementation of the ISO 31000 ERM system.

WHAT ARE AI RISK-CONTROL EXAMPLES?

The most important requirement for success of the ISO 31000 risk management framework is the active support of the Board of Directors and executive management. GM Board of Director's operational risk charter is shown on top of the page. Risk-control factors to consider in a successful AI design and implementation include the following:

- Obtain executive level support.

- Secure the views and opinions of stakeholders, customers, and interested humans.

- Understand enterprise context involving tribal knowledge, behavioral expectations, and hidden agendas.

- Develop a business case and plan for implementation based upon enterprise context.

AI Risk-Control Questions to Consider:

- Has a business case and implementation plan been developed?
- Is the executive sponsor directly involved in the architecture, design, implementation, and assurance of the risk management plan?
- Are Key Performance Indicators (KPI's) and KRI's (Key Risk Indicators) appropriate to the enterprise?
- Are accountabilities, responsibilities, and authorities clearly identified?

WHY IT MATTERS?

The human element is the biggest challenge in risk implementation. Why? Risk management involves RBPS and RBDM both of which involve adopting and adapting to new management, control, and other behavioral changes. Risk-based management requires new behaviors and attitudes.

CONTINUAL IMPROVEMENT OF RISK MANAGEMENT

Risk management facilitates continual improvement of the enterprise. Risk management has a strategic and tactical perspective that focuses on continual improvement including enhancing competitiveness and ensuring enterprise sustainability.

WHAT IS THE RISK?

ISO 31000 risk management is designed and implemented so it is used to facilitate continual improvement by humans including government, private companies, for profit companies, not for profit companies, and humans.

WHAT ARE AI RISK-CONTROL EXAMPLES?

Continual improvement of risk-controls is an overarching concept that incorporates the following:

- Meeting conformity assessment business and Quality Management System objectives.

- Monitoring variances in scope, quality, schedule, and costs.
- Ensuring KPI's and KRI's are achieved.
- Ensuring governance and statutory requirements are met.
- Improving RBPS and RBDM.
- Minimizing Volatility, Uncertainty, Complexity, and Ambiguity (VUCA).
- Improving upside risk management whether it is merger and acquisition activities, acquisition of capital equipment, undertaking new systems, and other activities.
- Improving the risk management framework and risk management system so it is cost effective.
- Integrating risk management processes into general management functions.

AI Risk-Control Questions to Consider:

- Are KPI's and KRI's continually improved?
- Does executive management have accountabilities and authorities for continuous improvement?
- Is executive compensation tied to continuous improvement objectives?
- Is continuous improvement a part of upside risk management?
- Is continuous improvement continually monitored?

WHY IT MATTERS?

Risk management is not static. Continual review of risks and risk-controls are required.

KEY POINTS

- AI principles are the basis of risk-based, problem-solving and decision-making.
- ISO 31000 is a risk management framework.
- The goal **of Trust Me: AI Risk Management** is to provide value to the reader.

ISO 31000 Risk Management Principles

- ISO 31000 offers 8 risk management principles useful for AI systems design and development.

- **Principle 1:** Risk management is an integral part of risk-based, problem-solving and decision-making.

- **Principle 2:** Risk management is systematic, structured, and timely.

- **Principle 3:** Risk management is tailored to the context and use case.

- **Principle 4:** Risk management is transparent, inclusive, and explainable.

- **Principle 5:** Risk management is dynamic, iterative, and responsive to change.

- **Principle 6:** Risk management is based on the best available information.

- **Principle 7:** Risk management takes human and cultural factors into account.

- **Principle 8:** Risk management facilitates continual improvement of the enterprise.

ISO 31000 RISK MANAGEMENT FRAMEWORK

WHAT IS THE KEY IDEA IN THIS CHAPTER?

Risk management framework is a set of processes and procedures that helps companies to identify, assess, and manage risks. The purpose of an ISO 31000 risk management framework is to help companies to make risk-based decisions and assure accountable and safe AI.

RISK MANAGEMENT FRAMEWORK

Risk management framework is a set of rules and processes that helps companies identify, assess, and manage risks.

WHAT IS THE RISK?

ISO 31000 is a risk management framework. It is important to have a risk management framework in place because it helps companies to:

- **Protect the AI information assets:** Risk management helps companies to identify and protect their assets such as their data, their employees, and their reputation.

- **Make smarter risk-based decisions:** Risk management helps companies to make risk-based decisions by providing them with information about the risks they face.

- **Reduce costs:** Risk management helps companies to reduce costs by preventing losses and by avoiding unnecessary expenses.

- **Ensure transparency:** Companies use risk management to assure that AI systems are transparent about how they make risk-based decisions. This can be done by providing information such as source code about the algorithms used in the system and by allowing humans to inspect the data used to train the system.

- **Provide accountability:** Companies use risk management to assure that a human is held accountable for the decisions made by AI systems. Creating a process for auditing AI systems and by assigning responsibility for the system to a human or group are critical for assuring accountability.

- **Assure fairness:** Companies use risk management to assure that AI systems are fair and unbiased in their risk-based decision-making. Monitoring the data used to train the system and by adjusting the system if it is found to be biased can assure fairness.

- **Secure individual privacy:** Companies use risk management to protect the privacy of the data used in AI systems. Encrypting the data, by limiting access to the data, and by deleting the data when it is no longer needed can help assure privacy.

- **Provide security:** Companies use risk management to protect AI systems from hacking and other security risks. Using secure software by implementing security controls and by monitoring the system for signs of attack provides a level of security.

WHAT ARE AI RISK-CONTROL EXAMPLES?

The purpose of the risk management framework is to assist the enterprise integrating risk management into critical processes, activities, and functions. This means that the framework is designed to fit the needs of the enterprise. **Trust Me: AI Risk Management** book describes aspects specific to the development, offering, or use of AI systems.

The risk owner is accountable for identifying and assessing these risk-controls such as developing and implementing risk mitigation strategies. This involves:

- **Threat modeling:** Threat modeling is a process of identifying potential threats to a system and developing risk mitigation strategies to reduce or eliminate these threats.

- **Risk analysis:** Risk analysis is a process of quantifying the likelihood and consequence of potential risks.

WHY IT MATTERS?

Risk management processes are the actions that companies take to identify, assess, and manage risks.

ISO 31000 RISK MANAGEMENT FRAMEWORK

Companies evaluate their risk management framework on an ongoing basis. This means assessing the effectiveness of the framework and making necessary changes to improve it.

WHAT IS THE RISK?

ISO 31000 standard provides guidance on evaluating risk management frameworks. This guidance includes the following:

- **Executive management assures that the enterprise's risk management framework is evaluated regularly:** This is done by setting up a process for evaluating the framework and by assigning responsibility for evaluation to a human or group.

- **Enterprise develops a plan for evaluating its risk management framework:** This plan includes a timeline for evaluation, a budget, and a list of criteria that are used to evaluate the framework.

- **Enterprise evaluates its risk management framework:** This involves using a variety of methods such as surveys, interviews, and focus groups. This assures that the evaluation is comprehensive and that stakeholders are involved.

- Enterprise uses the results of the evaluation to improve its risk management framework: This involves making changes to the framework's processes, systems, or risk-controls.

WHAT ARE AI RISK-CONTROL EXAMPLES?

The management within the enterprise is accountable for identifying, assessing, and treating risks. By following a risk management framework including risk-controls, companies assure that they are making smarter risk-based decisions and that they are managing risks effectively. By following this guidance, companies assure that they evaluate their risk management framework effectively.

WHY IT MATTERS?

Overall, by following the guidance provided in ISO 31000 and by taking the additional steps outlined above, companies assure that they have effective risk management in place. By following a risk management framework, companies protect their assets, and their reputation.

A risk management framework helps an enterprise by the following:

- Enterprise uses a risk management framework to identify potential risks to its business, such as financial risks, operational risks, and reputational risks.

- Enterprise uses a risk management framework to assess the likelihood and consequence of each risk. This information helps the enterprise to prioritize its risk mitigation efforts.

- Enterprise uses a risk management framework to develop and implement risk mitigation strategies. These strategies help the enterprise to reduce the likelihood or consequence of risks.

- Enterprise uses a risk management framework to monitor risks and to make sure that its risk mitigation strategies are effective. This information helps the enterprise to adjust its risk mitigation strategies as needed.

COMMUNICATION AND CONSULTATION

Communication and Consultation is the first step of the ISO 31000 risk management process. Communication and Consultation with stakeholders, customers, and interested occurs at each ISO 31000 risk management process step from Establishing the Context to Risk Treatment.

WHAT IS THE RISK?

Understanding the risk needs of key stakeholders, customers, and interested starts early so the purpose, intent, scope, extent, and objectives of the risk management process is designed, implemented, and assured.

WHAT ARE AI RISK-CONTROL EXAMPLES?

Effective Communication and Consultation establishes the basis for risk-based, problem-solving and risk-based, decision-making by key executives.

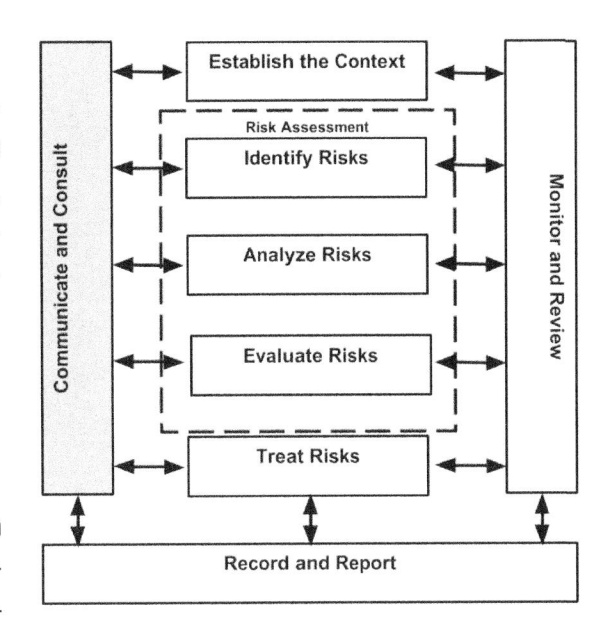

Communication and Consultation involves key risk-control inputs including:

- Identify environment, tone at the top, ethics, business model, and other key external and internal contextual factors.

- Ensure diverse points of view including stakeholders, customers, and interested are considered when defining risk criteria, attributes, risk appetite and other factors.

- Ensure executive management supports the risk management plan, risk management framework, risk management process, risk-controls, and risk treatment.

- Identify key stakeholders, customers, and interested involved with risk management and implementation of the ISO 31000 risk management process.

- Ensure the risks, needs, requirements, and expectations of stakeholders, customers, and interested humans are identified and are addressed.

- Ensure the KPI's, KRI's, and objectives are adequately identified.

- Ensure organization has knowledge, skills, and abilities to identify, analyze, control, and treat risks.

- Develop an effective communication and consultation plan for stakeholders, customers, and interested humans.

- Ensure effective change management throughout the application of the risk management process.

WHY IT MATTERS?

By following the guidance in ISO 31000, companies assure that they are communicating and consulting effectively with stakeholders. This assures that the AI system is developed that meets the needs of stakeholders and that minimizes risks.

ESTABLISHING THE CONTEXT

Establish the Context is the second step of the ISO 31000 risk management process.

WHAT IS THE RISK?

Defining the organizational context is the most important step in the risk management process.

The organizational context defines how the organization manages risk including Architecting, Designing, Deploying, and Assuring® risk. Finally, context is critical for setting the scope and risk criteria of the ISO 31000 risk management process.

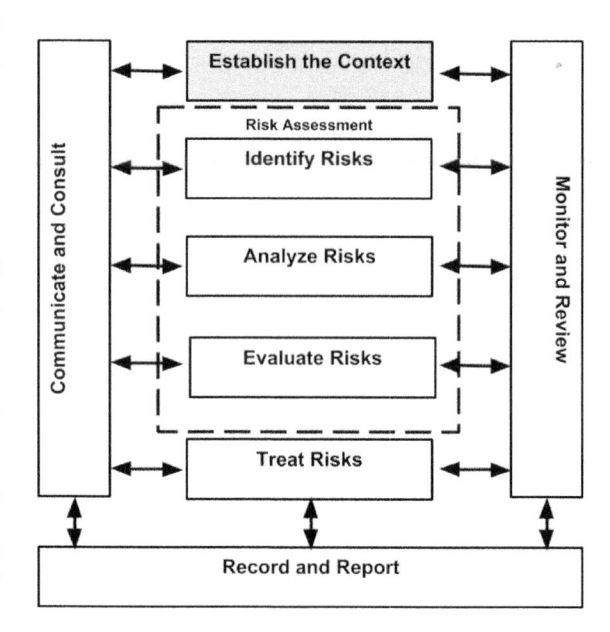

WHAT ARE AI RISK-CONTROL EXAMPLES?

Context is critical in the design and implementation of the ISO 31000 risk management framework, risk management processes, and risk-controls. When designing the framework, context determines which process steps are emphasized based on the organization's risk profile. An organization that produces heart monitors would design its framework differently than an organization that manufactures generic screws.

The risk management framework frames and defines the implementation of the ISO 31000 risk management process. The context defines the objectives, boundaries, scope, strategies, and tactics of the implementation of the risk management process.

WHY IT MATTERS?

Once the context is defined then approvals for resources, authorities, responsibilities, and accountabilities are defined.

RISK IDENTIFICATION

Risk Identification is the third step of the ISO 31000 risk management process.

WHAT IS THE RISK?

Risk Identification is the first process step of a risk assessment. ISO 31000 risk assessment consists of: 1. Risk identification; 2. Risk evaluation; and 3. Risk analysis.

ISO 31000 standard treats each one as a separate process step. Very often in practice, these three areas tend to morph and integrate into a risk assessment.

WHAT ARE AI RISK-CONTROL EXAMPLES?

Risk assessment is the main risk-based, problem-solving approach in ISO 31000. Complexity is closely linked with uncertainty. The nature, extent, and type of risks are dependent on organizational complexity. A system is composed of individual systems each of which has assemblies or subassemblies with multiple components of different levels of complexity.

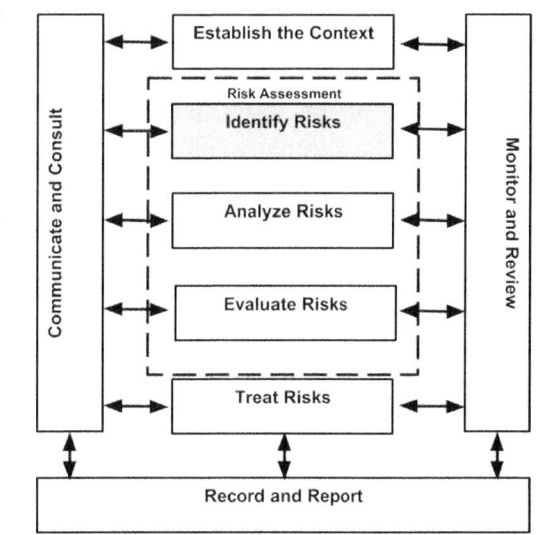

Conducting a risk assessment of a complex system is made difficult because there are cascading, interacting, dependent, and other risk interdependencies that make the risk assessment difficult. Risk assessment is done at the 1. Enterprise level; 2. Programmatic/Project/Process level; and 3. Transactional/Product level. Each level introduces additional complexity. Risk assessment also looks at present risk-control effectiveness.

Also, functional areas within an organization can be standalone areas where white space risks are important or unknown. Also, a company is organized around programs where each program has multiple independent and dependent systems with dependent, interdependent, and interactive risks. As well, risks are unknown or even unknowable.

WHY IT MATTERS?

Risk Identification processes are important for using AI systems safely and responsibly. By following these processes, companies assure that AI systems are used for good and not for harm.

RISK ANALYSIS

Risk Analysis is the fourth step of the ISO 31000 risk management process.

WHAT IS THE RISK?

ISO 31000 Risk Analysis is the second component of the risk assessment process. Risk Analysis involves understanding the type, extent, and nature of the threats and risks identified in the previous step.

Risk Analysis is important to determine if risks are treated or managed. As well, Risk Analysis determines the appropriate risk management strategies and methods.

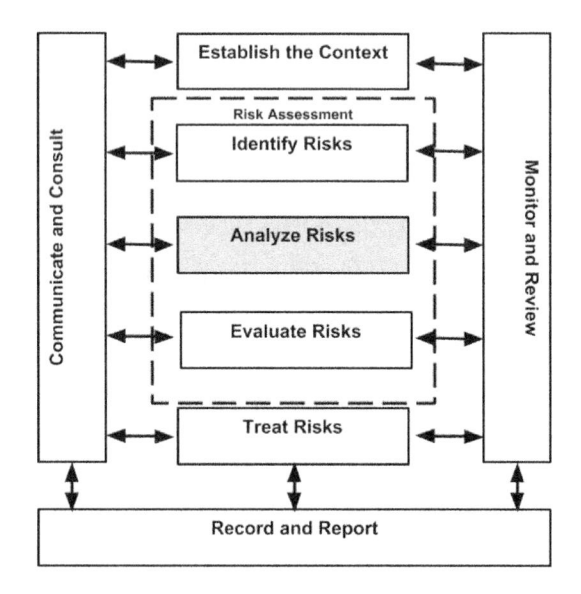

WHAT ARE AI RISK-CONTROL EXAMPLES?

Risk Analysis determines types of risk strategies, plans, tactics, and methods to implement in developing a risk-control structure, which involve:

- Risk Analysis is based upon organizational needs.

- RBPS and RBDM deal with uncertainty so the level of uncertainty is identified.

- Risk Analysis is based on organizational context, purpose of the analysis, requirements for reliability and accuracy, and purpose of the analysis. Higher risk assurance entails additional Risk Analysis.

- Type, level, extent, and nature of risk are analyzed.

- Risk Analysis reviews the causes and sources of threats, hazards, and risks.

- Risk Analysis considers both positive and negative impacts.

- Risk Analysis considers the likelihood of a consequence occurring.

- Risk consequences and likelihood are based on organizational risk sensitivity, context, economic impacts, environment, customer requirements, regulatory requirements and other factors.

- Depending upon these factors risk impacts are determined qualitatively or quantitatively.

- Consequences are determined based on organizational context.

- Factors that impact likelihood and consequences are identified.

- Events result in multiple impacts each of which has separate risks.

- Existing risk-control effectiveness and efficiency are analyzed.

- Consequences and likelihood of risk depend upon information availability, level of risk, and type of risk.

- Relationship, interdependence, cascading nature, correlation, and whitespace risks can impact Risk Analysis.

WHY IT MATTERS?

In this stage, the organization determines if the risk needs to be mitigated further.

RISK EVALUATION

Risk Evaluation is the fifth step of the ISO 31000 risk management process.

WHAT IS THE RISK?

The purpose of Risk Evaluation is to set up for risk-based, decision-making. The process step uses the quantitative and qualitative risk analysis generated in the preceding Analyze Risk process to prioritize risks at the 1. Enterprise level; 2. Programmatic/Project/Process level; and 3. Transactional/Product level.

WHAT ARE AI RISK-CONTROL EXAMPLES?

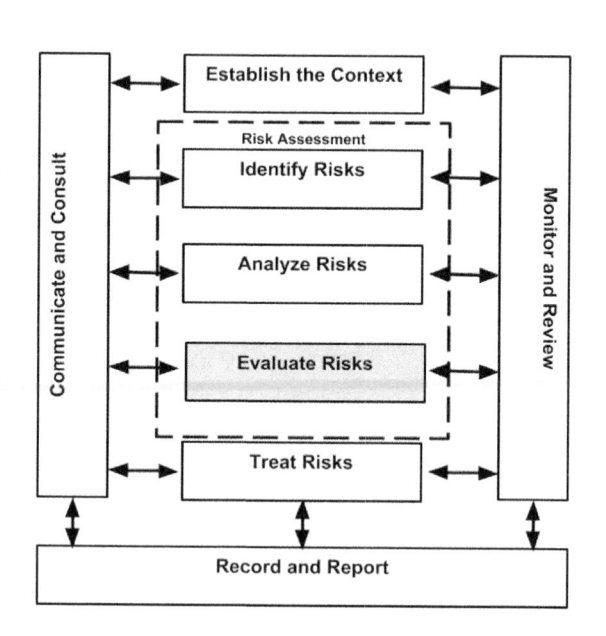

ISO 31000 Risk Evaluation compares the estimated consequence and likelihood of risk with the criteria defined when context was determined. Risk Evaluation helps to determine what type of risk treatment or management is required based on organizational risk appetite. If the current risk is within the organization's risk appetite, then additional risk-controls or treatment are not required. If the risk is greater than the risk appetite of the organization then additional treatment is required to bring risks within the organization's risk appetite.

Risk Evaluation process step does not try to identify and analyze every risk-control. The process step identifies critical risks that rise at the enterprise level. In prioritizing risks, it is critical to evaluate the organization's strategic direction and allocation of resources.

ISO 31000 ERM focuses on treating the few critical risks that result in a dramatic reduction in residual risk, systemic risk, material risk, AI risk, whitespace risk, dependency risk, dependency risk and chronic risk.

In this process risk step, executive leadership reviews enterprise risks as well as information on how risks are controlled and treated. Executive leadership is prepared to dedicate resources to minimizing these risks. Executive leadership revisits organizational risk appetite and programmatic risk tolerances considering the enterprise risk portfolio and make required changes.

WHY IT MATTERS?

Risk treatment takes into account the external context including regulations, environment, and customer requirements. External stakeholders, customers, and interested humans have different risk appetites that are considered in the evaluation of risk. Risk Evaluation determined whether to accept the risk and retain existing risk-controls based upon the organization's risk attitude, criteria, and acceptance.

RISK TREATMENT

Risk Treatment is the sixth step of the ISO 31000 risk management process.

WHAT IS THE RISK?

In this risk-based, decision-making step, the basic idea of Risk Treatment is to control risks within the organization's risk appetite.

The process step looks at the range of Risk Treatment options and prepares control plans for the selected treatment option. Risk Treatment process step reviews opportunities, taking upside risks to achieve mission critical success as well as efforts to minimize the adverse impact of downside risk.

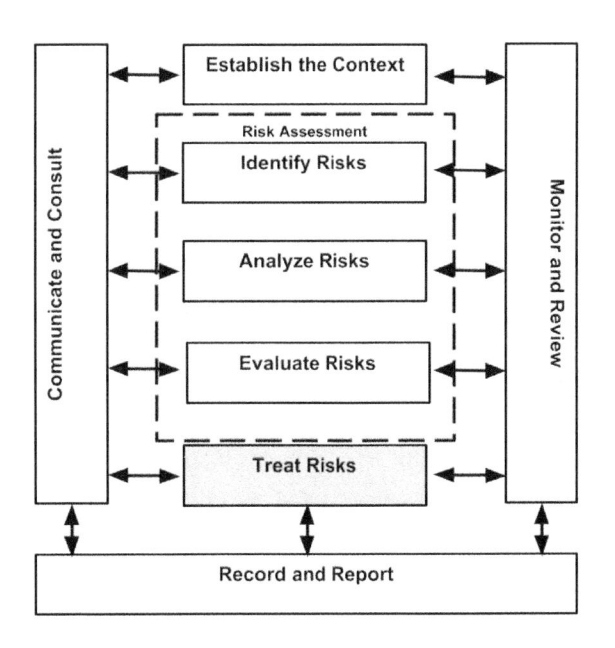

WHAT ARE AI RISK-CONTROL EXAMPLES?

Using a prioritized list of qualified risk requirements, executive management evaluates treatment options using a value weighted, evaluation process. The purpose is to ensure appropriate risk-based decisions are made and resources are allocated to programs, systems, and processes based on organizational risk appetite and tolerance.

Risk Treatment involves the design of the control environment including risk-controls for the organization. Risk Treatment is a cyclical process of assessing the effectiveness, efficiency, and economics of the application of a risk-control or Risk Treatment and determining whether the residual risk is within the organization's risk appetite.

WHY IT MATTERS?

Risk Treatment is the key step where additional risk-controls are applied to the organization.

MONITOR AND REVIEW

Monitor and Review is the seventh step of the ISO 31000 risk management process.

WHAT IS THE RISK?

Monitor and Review is a critical part of risk assurance. Monitor and Review is part of ongoing surveillance of the ISO 31000 risk management process to determine its effectiveness, efficiency, and economics.

Risk management is an important part of using AI systems safely and responsibly. By following the principles and processes of risk management, companies assure that AI is used for good and not for harm. By understanding the risks and benefits of AI systems, companies make risk-based decisions about using them.

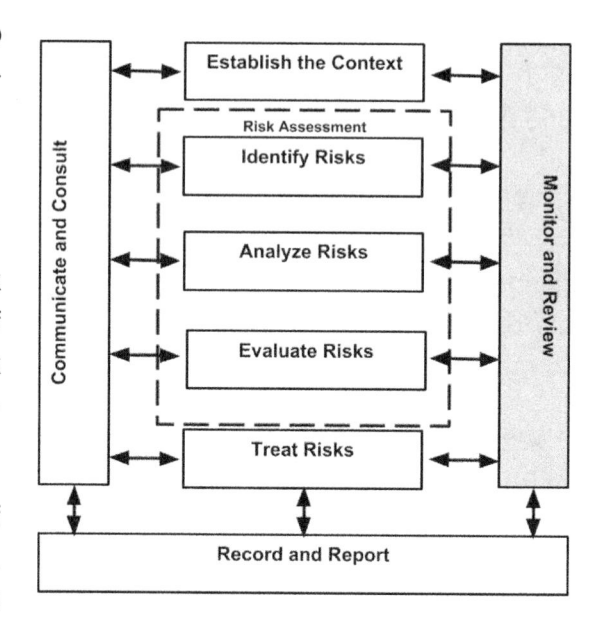

WHAT ARE AI RISK-CONTROL EXAMPLES?

Monitor and Review is a continual effort to ensure the appropriate treatment and risk-controls are applied within the organizational risk appetite. It is necessary repeat the Monitor and Review cycle regularly with each step in the ISO 31000 risk management process.

Monitor and Review provides important benchmarking data against actual ISO 31000 ERM risk management outcomes, business objectives, expected outcomes, residual risk, budget, and performance levels.

Monitor and Review accountabilities, responsibilities, and authorities are defined and documented. The process step measures actual progress against milestones, which provide important KPI and KRI performance metrics that are incorporated into the organization's performance management and improvement processes.

The process step monitors and reviews status of risks, risk-controls, treatment, and residual risks at the 1. Enterprise level; 2. Programmatic/Project/Process level; and 3. Product Transactional level. The purpose of this process step is to assure management treatment strategies and risk-controls remain effective, efficient, and economic.

Once the risk is within the organization's risk appetite or tolerance, then there is a continuous process of monitoring and review of the status of each process step as well as the treatment of risks.

Monitor and Review processes are integrated into each component of the risk management framework and elements of the ISO 31000 risk management process.

WHY IT MATTERS?

Benefits of Monitor and Review include:

- Ensure appropriate application of Risk-Based Thinking involving RBPS and RBDM.
- Validate assumptions about the criteria, context, environment, and other factors are still appropriate.

- Institute a change management process if assumptions and context have changed.

- Assure expected business objectives are met and achieved.

- Ensure risk-controls are effective, efficient, and economic.

- Capture information to improve the design, implementation, and assurance of the risk management process.

- Assess events, risks, hazards, trends, changes, successes, and failures.

- Monitor changes in the context, risk management framework, stakeholder requirements, risk criteria, and risk appetite, which requires additional risk torment and management.

- Ensure results of the risk assessment are within the risk appetite of the organization.

- Assure risk assessment has been properly applied.

- Ensure authority, accountability, and responsibility of Monitor and Review are periodically updated.

- Identify emerging risks.

- Identify new opportunities for investment

- Prepare reports to executive management.

- Ensure risk assurance is appropriate to the organizational risk appetite.

- Prepare reports to the Board of Directors and other risk information stakeholders.

DEPLOYING THE ISO 31000 RMF

Companies adapt their risk management framework to changes in the enterprise's environment, such as changes in technology, regulations, or markets.

WHAT IS THE RISK?

Companies need to implement their risk management framework. This means putting in place the necessary processes, systems, and risk-controls to manage risks effectively.

ISO 31000 standard provides guidance on implementing risk management frameworks. This guidance includes the following:

- Executive management assures that the enterprise's risk management framework is implemented effectively. This is done by providing the necessary resources and support for implementation.

- Enterprise develops a plan for implementing its risk management framework. This plan includes a timeline for implementation, a budget, and a list of tasks that are completed.

- Enterprise implements its risk management framework in stages. This assures that the framework is implemented effectively and that any problems that arise are identified and addressed.

- Enterprise monitors the effectiveness of its risk management framework on an ongoing basis. This assures that the framework is meeting the enterprise's needs and that it is used effectively.

By following this guidance, companies assure that they implement their risk management framework effectively.

WHAT ARE AI RISK-CONTROL EXAMPLES?

The International Organization for Standardization (ISO) provides guidance on improvement through its ISO 31000 standard. The guidance includes these risk-controls:

- **Executive management:** Executive management assures that the enterprise's risk management framework is improved regularly. This is done by setting up a process for improvement and by assigning responsibility for improvement to a human or group.

- **Risk management plans:** Enterprise develops a plan for improving its risk management framework. This plan includes a timeline for improvement, a budget and a list of criteria that are used to evaluate the framework.

- **Risk management monitoring:** Enterprise improves its risk management framework using a variety of methods such as surveys, interviews, and focus groups. This assures that the improvement is comprehensive and that stakeholders are involved.

- **Improve risk management framework:** The enterprise uses the results of the evaluation to improve its risk management framework. This involves making changes to the framework's processes, systems, or risk-controls.

WHY IT MATTERS?

Companies assure that they improve their risk management framework effectively. Overall, by following the guidance provided in ISO 31000 and by taking the additional steps outlined above, companies assure that they have effective risk management in place

AI RMF IMPROVEMENT

Companies improve their AI risk management framework (AI RMF) on an ongoing basis. This means making changes to the framework to assure that it is meeting the enterprise's needs and that it is used effectively.

WHAT IS THE RISK?

ISO is developing a new management system standard for AI called ISO 42001. ISO describes the purpose of the new standard as addressing the following:

- "The relative transparency and explainability of automated decision systems.

- The use of outputs such as data analysis from Machine Learning systems, which are trained from data, once or continuously, and adapt to changes in its inputs. This differs from traditional procedural programming, since an AI system may change its behaviour over the course of its use.

- The degree of autonomy of an AI system as in autonomous driving vehicles."[27]

WHAT ARE AI RISK-CONTROL EXAMPLES?

This risk-control guidance includes the following:

- Executive management assures that the enterprise's risk management framework is continually improved. This is done by setting up a process for continual improvement and by assigning responsibility for continual improvement to a human or group.

- Enterprise develops a plan for continually improving its risk management framework. This plan includes a timeline for continual improvement, a budget, and a list of criteria that is used to evaluate the framework.

- Enterprise continually improves its risk management framework using a variety of methods, such as surveys, interviews, and focus groups. This assures that the continual improvement is comprehensive and that stakeholders are involved.

- Enterprise uses the results of the evaluation to continually improve its risk management framework. This involved making changes to the framework's processes, systems, or risk-controls.

WHY IT MATTERS?

Companies assure that they continually improve their risk management framework effectively.

KEY POINTS

- ISO 31000 is a commonly used risk management framework.

- This book is based on ISO 31000, ISO 42001, and other risk management frameworks.

- Risk management processes are the actions that companies take to identify, assess, and manage risks.

- AI involves many social-technical technologies such as engineering, development, statistics, programming, and social sciences.

- AI RMF implementation is tailored to the context of the organization.

- AI RMF needs to evaluated any time there is a major change in the AI system.

- AI is improved on an ongoing basis due to changes in context, data, and requirements.

- AI RMF deployment considers executive management, plans, monitoring, and stakeholder needs.

- Companies need a process for identifying, assessing, and treating risks.

- AI RMF management is a hierarchy of enterprise system level risk-controls, programmatic/process/project, and transactional/product risk-controls.

- Communications are integrated into every element of the AI RMF.

AI RISK PRINCIPLES

WHAT IS THE KEY IDEA IN THIS CHAPTER?

AI trust involves many of its characteristics that are based on context. In this chapter, we discuss many elements of trust including: fairness, safety, privacy, robustness, transparency, environmental friendliness, traceability, and maintainability.

IMPORTANCE OF AI TRUST

WHAT IS THE RISK?

Joanna Bryson distills the importance of trust:

> "Trust is a relationship between peers in which the trusting party, while not knowing for certain what the trusted party will do, believes any promises being made. AI is a set of system development techniques that allow machines to compute actions or knowledge from a set of data. ...
>
> Many claim that such accountability is impossible with AI, because of its complexity, or the fact that it includes machine learning or has some sort of autonomy. humans have been holding many human-run institutions such as banks and governments accountable for centuries. The humans in these institutions learn and have autonomy, and the workings of their brains are far inscrutable than any system deliberately built and maintained by humans."[28]

WHAT ARE AI RISK-CONTROL EXAMPLES?

Forbes Magazine and many other news outlets say that AI's biggest problem is trust.[29] To trust AI, the following risk-controls at a minimum are required:

- Use of a risk management framework and AI lifecycle to develop and deploy the AI product.

- Define 'what is' AI standards against which to assess, assure, comply, and adhere to.

- Follow 'how to' standards to assess, account, and assure the AI system.

- Define 'who' standards on knowledge, skills, and abilities for the experts to conduct the AI assessments and assurance.

WHY IT MATTERS?

Salesforce survey identifies why 'trust matters':

> "Out of the 14,000 respondents surveyed, 76% said they trust companies to make honest claims about their products and services but nearly 50% claimed they do not trust them to use AI ethically.
>
> While they highlighted multiple concerns, the most prominent challenges they reported were the lack of transparency and the lack of a human in the loop to validate the output of the AI — demanded by more than 80%. Just 37% of the respondents said they actually trust AI to provide as accurate responses as a human would."[30]

AI SYSTEM RISKS

AI management objectives focus on identifying and reducing risks related to AI technologies. This includes potential biases, security vulnerabilities, legal compliance, and unintended consequences. Setting objectives for risk management ensures that AI systems are developed with appropriate safeguards in place.

WHAT IS THE RISK?

AI systems bring new or unexpected risks to a company. This means that they might introduce new risks that the company never faced before or they change the likelihood of existing risks. An AI system used to decide who gets a loan could create a new risk of discrimination. This is achieved by following the principles of AI risk management and taking actions to minimize the risks.

WHAT ARE AI RISK-CONTROL EXAMPLES?

This book lists 100's of risk-controls to manage and mitigate AI risks. However, simple steps to manage AI system risk include:

- **Use representative data:** Companies use data that represents the diverse population the AI system will interact with. This reduces the risk of biased data influencing the AI's decisions.

- **Design fair algorithms:** Algorithms are designed to be fair and unbiased. This helps reduce the risk of algorithmic bias, which could lead to unfair outcomes.

- **Implement security measures:** Putting strong security measures in place helps protect AI systems from hacking and other security risks. This lowers the risk of unauthorized access or malicious attacks on the AI system.

WHY IT MATTERS?

The companies commit to investing in cybersecurity and insider threat safeguards to protect proprietary and unreleased models. These models are an essential part of an AI system. Companies agree that it is vital that the model be released only when intended and when security risks are considered.

Companies commit to facilitating third-party discovery and reporting of vulnerabilities in their AI systems. Issues can persist even after an AI system is released and a robust reporting mechanism allows them to be found and fixed quickly.

AI TRUSTWORTHINESS

Trustworthiness is how reliable and dependable an AI system is in performing its intended function safely and securely. It is essential to consider trustworthiness when developing or using AI systems because they have a critical impact on humans.

WHAT IS THE RISK?

Trustworthy AI involves various aspects, such as:

- **Identifying and assessing AI risks:** This means recognizing potential risks to trustworthiness like bias, privacy concerns, and security vulnerabilities.

- **Mitigating AI risks:** Taking measures to reduce the chances of AI risks impacting trustworthiness and minimizing their impacts if they occur.

- **Monitoring and improving trustworthiness:** Continuously evaluating the performance of AI systems and making necessary improvements.

By addressing these aspects, companies establish AI risk criteria suitable for their specific needs.

WHAT ARE AI RISK-CONTROL EXAMPLES?

Examples of how risk-controls enhance trustworthiness include:

- **Using transparent and accountable processes:** This builds trust with stakeholders as they understand how AI systems work and make risk-based decisions.

- **Protecting personal data:** Ensuring that personal information is kept safe and not misused.

- **Securing AI systems:** Preventing unauthorized access to AI systems, safeguarding them from potential attacks.

- **Testing and evaluating AI systems:** Regularly assessing AI performance to make sure it functions as intended.

WHY IT MATTERS?

The ultimate goal is to ensure that AI systems are trusted to act, decide, and problem-solve ethically and responsibly. This fosters confidence among users and humans making AI technology safer and beneficial for everyone.

AI RISK CRITERIA

AI risk criteria are measures or standards used to evaluate and manage potential risks linked to AI systems.

WHAT IS THE RISK?

They help assess the possible negative impacts, unintended consequences, or vulnerabilities of AI. These criteria cover factors like fairness, safety, privacy, security, transparency, interpretability, accountability, and societal impact.

WHAT ARE AI RISK-CONTROL EXAMPLES?

Risk-control criteria to consider include:

- **Nature and type of uncertainties:** This involves understanding the likelihood and consequences of AI risks occurring.

- **Potential for harm:** AI systems cause harm to humans, property, or the environment, which are physical, psychological, or economic in nature.

- **Objectives impacted:** These include both tangible and intangible objectives that could be influenced by AI systems.

- **Likelihood of harm:** The probability of AI systems causing harm depends on how they are designed and implemented. An AI system controlling a self-driving car poses higher risks compared to one used for product recommendations.

- **Potential for unintended consequences:** AI systems lead to unexpected outcomes such as discrimination or bias, which impact humans.

- **Cost of mitigating AI risk:** The expense of reducing AI risks vary depending on the system's complexity. Implementing safety features in a self-driving car, It would be costly than doing so in a product recommendation system.

- **Available resources to mitigate AI risks:** This includes time, money, and other resources that are allocated to minimize AI risks.

WHY IT MATTERS?

Considering these criteria helps companies assess AI risks and act appropriately to mitigate them. Regulators want to ensure that AI is developed and used so that it benefits humans while minimizing potential risks.

ACCOUNTABLE AI

An essential aspect of AI development is socially responsibility and accountability.

WHAT IS THE RISK?

Socially responsible AI according to Lu Cheng, Kush Varshney, and Huan Liu (Academic researchers) is:

> "Social responsibility of AI refers to a human value-driven process where values such as fairness, transparency, accountability, reliability and safety, privacy and security, and inclusiveness are the principles; designing socially responsible AI algorithms is the means; and addressing the social expectations of generating shared value enhancing both AI's ability and benefits to society is the main objective."[31]

WHAT ARE AI RISK-CONTROL EXAMPLES?

One global standard that helps guide companies in being socially responsible is ISO 26000. ISO 26000 - Social Responsibility Standard: ISO 26000 provides guidelines for being socially responsible focusing on these core risk-controls:

- **Enterprise governance:** This deals with how a company is managed and controlled, including being transparent, accountable, and ethical in its behavior.

- **Human rights:** This involves respecting the rights of everyone involved like employees, customers, suppliers, and the community.

- **Labor practices:** This involves ensuring fair treatment and respect for employees covering aspects like fair wages, safe working conditions, and the right to join associations.

- **Environment:** This involves taking actions to protect the environment and reduce the company's impacts such as addressing pollution, managing waste, and tackling climate change.

- **Fair operating practices:** This means conducting business in a fair and ethical manner including practices related to competition, pricing, and marketing.

- **Consumer issues:** This involves protecting consumer interests through safe products, transparent information, and proper ways to resolve issues.

- **Community involvement:** This means collaborating with the community to improve quality of life, engaging in social investment, volunteering, and community development.

- **Development:** This means reducing poverty and inequality through sustainable development, corporate social responsibility, and social entrepreneurship.

- **Transparency:** AI systems are complex making it hard to understand how they work.

- **Accountability:** A human is held accountable for the decisions made by AI systems. It could be a human or a group of humans.

- **Fairness:** AI systems are fair and unbiased when making decisions. They do not discriminate against humans based on their race, gender, age, or other factors.

- **Privacy:** AI systems protect the data they use and not share it with other humans without permission.

- **Security:** AI systems are secure from hacking and other security risks to prevent data theft or damage.

WHY IT MATTERS?

Using ISO 26000 helps companies manage AI risk responsibly and ethically making a positive impact on humans while developing AI technologies.

Humans understand the political, social, technical, and other responsibilities of AI to use it responsibly and ensure it benefits humans without causing harm.

SOCIETAL IMPLICATIONS OF AI

When AI systems are developed, they have an impact on humans and politics.

WHAT IS THE RISK?

AI can be misused to create fake news, discriminate against certain groups, and invade humans' privacy. It is crucial for companies to be aware of these potential AI risks and take action to reduce them.

Building good relationships with external stakeholders is essential for companies. This means understanding what AI stakeholders value, what they need, and what they expect. Stakeholders might be worried about how AI is used, so it is vital for companies to be open and transparent about their AI practices.

WHAT ARE AI RISK-CONTROL EXAMPLES?

The use of AI impacts a company's ability to fulfill its contractual obligations and risk-control promises. This is because AI systems are always learning and changing making it challenging to guarantee that they will meet a company's commitments.

When companies design and create AI systems and services, they consider the scope of their contracts and relationships. AI systems are complex and involve multiple stakeholders. Companies need to decide who owns the data used to develop AI systems.

WHY IT MATTERS?

Companies understand the social responsibilities and public impacts of AI to ensure they use AI in an accountable and ethical manner.

AI FAIRNESS

AI systems have the power to make risk-based decisions that influence human lives.

AI Risk Principles

WHAT IS THE RISK?

These risk-based decisions are unfair if they are based on inaccurate or biased data. Reasons why AI systems are unfair:

- **Bias in the data:** If the data used to train the AI system is biased, the results will likely be biased too. If a loan approval AI system is trained on data that favors white and male humans, it will tend to approve loans for similar humans.

- **Bias in the humans who build and use the systems:** The humans who develop and use AI systems introduce their biases into the system. If the team of engineers building the AI system is mostly white and male, they might unintentionally create a biased system.

WHAT ARE AI RISK-CONTROL EXAMPLES?

To ensure fairness, companies take several risk-control steps:

- **Using accurate and unbiased data:** They use diverse and representative data when training AI systems.

- **Using fair and unbiased algorithms:** They ensure that the algorithms avoid bias and undergo testing to confirm their fairness.

- **Monitoring for bias:** Companies monitor keep an eye on their AI systems for any signs of bias in the results.

- **Taking action to mitigate bias:** If bias is detected, companies work to minimize it, like retraining the system with better data or modifying algorithms.

WHY IT MATTERS?

Companies make sure their AI systems are fair and unbiased by following the steps in this book.

AI SECURITY RISKS

AI systems are becoming widespread, but this brings a new set of security risks related to AI.

WHAT IS THE RISK?

Examples of these security risks include:

- **Data poisoning:** When a human intentionally corrupts the data used to train an AI system causing it to produce incorrect or biased results.

- **Adversarial attacks:** Intentionally trying to trick an AI system into making a mistake by crafting input data or adversarial machine learning techniques.

- **Model stealing:** Attempting to steal the code or data used to train an AI system, allowing them to create its own AI system that is better than the original.

WHAT ARE AI RISK-CONTROL EXAMPLES?

To protect against AI security risks, companies can take the following risk-control actions:

- **Secure data collection and storage:** Encrypting data both at rest and in transit and using strong authentication and authorization mechanisms.

- **Training AI systems on accurate and unbiased data:** Using data cleaning techniques to remove errors or biases from the data.

- **Implementing security measures against adversarial attacks:** Using input validation and output verification techniques to prevent attackers from tricking the system.

- **Implementing security measures against model stealing:** Using techniques like watermarking to make it difficult for attackers to steal the code or data used to train the system.

WHY IT MATTERS?

Companies protect their AI systems from security risks by focusing on precautions listed in this chapter.

AI SAFETY

AI systems are used to control Internet Of Things machines and devices but this can introduce new safety risks.

WHAT IS THE RISK?

Examples of these safety risks include:

- **Accidents:** AI systems make mistakes that lead to accidents and injuries.
- **Malfunctions:** AI systems malfunction resulting in injuries or even death.
- **Hacking:** AI systems can be hacked and used to cause harm to humans or property.

WHAT ARE AI RISK-CONTROL EXAMPLES?

To mitigate these AI safety risks, companies take the following risk-control actions:

- **Design AI and IOT systems with safety in mind:** Using safety-critical design and fault tolerance techniques to ensure safer functioning.
- **Thoroughly test AI systems:** Testing the systems for accuracy, reliability, and safety before implementation.
- **Monitor AI systems in operation:** Continuously monitoring the systems to detect signs of malfunction or hacking.
- **Have a plan for dealing with accidents or malfunctions:** Developing procedures to evacuate humans from the area, provide medical attention to the injured, and investigate the cause of the accident or malfunction especially for safety-critical and humans-critical systems.

WHY IT MATTERS?

Companies educate their employees about AI safety risks and how to mitigate them, ensuring safer system usage and reducing potential harm to humans and property.

PERSONAL PRIVACY

Privacy is about having control over the information related to a human – who collects it, stores it, processes it, and who has access to it. Protecting personal privacy is now a law in most developed countries. AI regulations are piggy backed on privacy laws in the near future.

WHAT IS THE RISK?

Here are ways AI systems can impact privacy:

- **Identity theft:** If personal information is stolen, they could steal a human's identity causing financial problems and difficulty getting loans or jobs.

- **Discrimination:** If a bad actor obtains health information, it could be used to discriminate leading to job or insurance denials.

- **Harassment:** Personal information in the wrong hands could be used for harassment such as sending threatening messages.

- **Personal data collection:** AI systems collect various data about personal information, location data, and browsing history.

- **Personal data storage:** This data is stored for a long time even after stopping using the AI system.

- **Personal data processing:** AI systems use a human's data to make predictions about future behavior or likelihood of committing a crime.

- **Data disclosure:** AI systems share data with third party humans like advertisers or law enforcement.

- **Data mining:** AI systems mine data for personal information like names, addresses, and phone numbers.

- **Electronic stalking:** AI systems track movements and activities.

WHAT ARE AI RISK-CONTROL EXAMPLES?

To protect privacy, companies can take these risk-control steps:

- Comply with national privacy laws.
- Follow privacy standards.
- Collect only necessary data for the AI system's purpose.
- Store data securely and for the shortest possible time.
- Use data only for its intended purpose.
- Do not share data with third party humans without a person's consent.

WHY IT MATTERS?

When using AI systems, it is crucial to protect privacy by safeguarding data and preventing unwarranted access. Otherwise, costly litigation can ensue.

AI ROBUSTNESS

AI systems may not be very strong and reliable because they are made of neural networks, which are complex and hard to understand. These neural networks make unexpected mistakes or even crash.

WHAT IS THE RISK?

Robustness in AI means a system does its job even when things are not perfect. A car is robust if it drives safely even with flat tires or imperfect brakes. While this analogy is not perfect, it highlights the importance of having robust AI systems when certain elements of the AI do not work.

WHAT ARE AI RISK-CONTROL EXAMPLES?

To make AI systems robust, there are a few things that can be done. One is using training data, which helps the neural network learn to handle unexpected situations. Another is neural network's performance.

Companies make AI systems more robust by:

- **Using ample training data:** Data helps the neural network perform better in unexpected situations.

- **Employing advanced algorithms:** Sophisticated algorithms enhance the neural network's robustness.

- **Thoroughly testing the AI system:** Before deployment, it is crucial to test the AI system in various conditions.

- **Monitoring the AI system:** Once deployed, constant monitoring is essential to detect any potential problems.

WHY IT MATTERS?

Ensuring AI systems are robust is critical to their successful and reliable performance. Achieving perfect robustness in AI is challenging. AI systems will still have weaknesses and may not handle unexpected situations. That is why it is vital to design AI systems with robustness in mind from the beginning.

AI EXPLAINABILITY

Explainability is the ability to understand why an AI system made a particular risk-based decision. This is important for stakeholders who trust the AI system and understand how it works.

AI systems often make risk-based decisions without human input. This is helpful for tasks that are repetitive or time-consuming. It is important for AI systems to be transparent and explainable. This means that humans understand and explain how the AI system works and why it made a particular risk-based decision.

WHAT IS THE RISK?

The importance of AI explainability lies in several aspects. First, it helps humans trust AI systems to make fair and accurate risk-based decisions. Second, it allows humans to understand why the system made a specific risk-based decision and whether it was fair.

If an AI system is used to make risk-based decisions about who gets a loan, the human is able to understand how the system makes these decisions. Humans know the factors the system considers and how much weight it assigns to each factor. Stakeholders can identify situations where human oversight is necessary. This means they review the decisions made by the AI system and ensure they are fair and accurate. Stakeholders define criteria for fairness and identify any bias in the AI system.

WHAT ARE AI RISK-CONTROL EXAMPLES?

If an enterprise cannot explain how its AI system works, humans cannot trust it. They cannot hold the enterprise accountable for the risk-based decisions made by the system.

Explainability is about being able to explain how an AI system makes risk-based decisions. This can help explain why the system made a certain risk-based decision and whether or not the decision was fair.

If an AI system is used to make risk-based decisions about who gets a loan, humans understand how the system makes its decisions. They know what risk-control factors the system considers and how much emphasis it gives to each factor.

Stakeholders can identify where human oversight is needed. This means that AI risk-based decisions are fair and accurate. Stakeholders can define fairness criteria and identify bias in the AI system.

Importance of AI Explainability

Explainability is important for the following reasons:

- **Trust AI systems:** If humans understand how an AI system works, they are likely to trust it to make risk-based decisions that are fair and accurate.

- **Use AI systems effectively:** If humans understand how an AI system works, they use it to their advantage. For example, they use it to make smarter risk-based decisions or to find new opportunities.

- **Hold companies accountable for the risk-based decisions made by AI systems:** If humans understand how an AI system works, they can hold companies accountable for the risk-based decisions that the system makes.

Too Much Explainability

There are AI risks with possibly too much explainability:

- **Privacy AI risks:** If too much information about how an AI system works is made public, then private information may be at risk.

- **Security AI risks:** If too much information about how an AI system works is made available to unauthorized humans, then the system can be hacked.

- **Confidentiality AI risks:** If too much information about how an AI system works is shared with humans who do not have access to it, then it could be compromised.

- **Intellectual property AI risks:** If too much information about how an AI system works is shared with competitors, then it could be used for IP theft.

WHY IT MATTERS?

Explainability matters as it helps humans understand the reasons behind AI system decisions, promoting trust, effectiveness, and accountability while considering potential risks and taking appropriate action to manage them.

If companies cannot explain how their AI systems work, humans cannot trust them. It means humans cannot hold these companies accountable for the risk-based decisions made by their AI systems.

AI TRANSPARENCY

Transparency and explainability are similar concepts. They are important for AI systems because they allow humans to understand how the systems work and to trust them.

WHAT IS THE RISK?

Transparency is about sharing information about how an AI system works. This helps to explain the system makes risk-based decisions and why it might make certain choices. Transparency is about providing information about the AI system such as its capabilities and limitations.

Transparency and explainability are similar concepts that are crucial for AI systems because they allow humans to understand how these systems work and build trust in them. Transparency means sharing information about how an AI system operates, helping humans understand how it makes risk-based decisions and why it chooses certain options. By providing details about the system's capabilities and limitations, transparency allows humans to make informed decisions about whether to use the AI system.

WHAT ARE AI RISK-CONTROL EXAMPLES?

There are ways to achieve risk-control transparency and explainability in AI systems. One approach is to use simpler algorithms that are easier to understand. Another way is to provide information about the data used to train the system. Developers create tools that assist humans in understanding how the system functions.

Transparency is important for a number of reasons:

- **Trust AI systems:** If humans understand how an AI system works, they are likely to trust it to make risk-based decisions that are fair and accurate.

- **Use AI systems effectively:** If humans understand how an AI system works, they will use it to their advantage. They use it to make smarter decisions or to find new opportunities.

- **Hold companies accountable for the risk-based decisions made by AI systems**: If humans understand how an AI system works, they will hold companies accountable for the risk-based decisions that the system makes.

WHY IT MATTERS?

There is a balance between transparency and protecting privacy, security, confidentiality, and intellectual property. Excessive transparency leads to AI risks, such as privacy issues if too much information about how an AI system works becomes public or security risks if unauthorized humans access this information. It could pose confidentiality risks if sensitive information is shared with those who should not have access or intellectual property risks if competitors gain access to valuable AI system details.

By making AI systems transparent and explainable, developers foster trust and allow effective use of these systems. The level of transparency and explainability required for an AI system varies based on its purpose, type, and regulatory demands. An AI system making medical decisions may need more transparency and explainability than an AI system recommending movies.

Transparency and explainability are crucial for AI systems as they allow humans to understand how the systems make risk-based decisions. This understanding empowers humans to make informed decisions about whether to use these systems effectively.

ENVIRONMENTAL FRIENDLY AI

AI systems have both positive and negative impacts on the environment. On the positive side, AI systems are beneficial for the environment. They help reduce pollution and enhance efficiency in various ways. By optimizing traffic flow, AI systems decrease emissions and improve fuel efficiency, which is good for the environment. AI systems play a crucial role in developing new technologies that protect the environment like renewable energy sources such as solar and wind power.

WHAT IS THE RISK?

There are negative impacts with AI systems and the environment. One major concern is the amount of energy required during the training and operation of AI systems. The training phase of large language models consume an enormous amount of energy that can have adverse effects on the environment.

WHAT ARE AI RISK-CONTROL EXAMPLES?

It is important to reduce the environmental impact of AI systems. It is important to consider the environmental impacts of AI systems when developing and using these systems. By making informed risk-control choices, it can be assured so that AI is used so that it benefits the environment.

Positive impacts:

- **AI systems are used to reduce pollution and improve efficiency:** AI systems are used to optimize energy systems, which reduce emissions.

- **AI systems are used to develop new technologies that protect the environment:** AI systems are used to develop new renewable energy sources such as solar and wind power.

Negative impacts:

- **Training and operation of AI systems consume a lot of energy:** The training phase of a large language model requires as much energy as driving a car for thousands of miles.

- **Data used to train AI systems come from sources that harm the environment:** AI systems are trained on data that is collected from social media, which can contribute to the spread of misinformation and hate speech.

WHY IT MATTERS?

To address these concerns, it is crucial to be mindful of the environmental impacts of AI systems during their development and usage. Making informed decisions help ensure that AI is used minimizing its negative effects and maximizing its positive contributions.

AI DATA QUALITY

Many AI techniques, such as deep learning, highly depend on big data since their accuracy relies on the amount of data they have. The misuse or disclosure data particularly personal and sensitive data, such as health records, could have harmful effects on humans, thus privacy protection has become a major concern in big data analysis in AI.

WHAT IS THE RISK?

The data needs to be accurate and complete for the AI system to work properly. Stakeholders can minimize AI risks with proper data collection, processing, and use. If an AI system is used to diagnose diseases, the data used to train the AI system needs to be accurate. If the data is not accurate, the AI system might make incorrect diagnoses. Stakeholders can help identify and address these AI risks.

AI systems like deep learning need a lot of data to work. This data can be about anything like what sites does a human visit or what is bought. This data can be personal, like health records or bank account information. If This data is misused or disclosed, it could harm a human and that's why privacy protection is so important when using AI systems.

The complexity of generative AI technologies make it difficult to explain how an AI system works. Stakeholders help by providing feedback and insights into the AI system. This can help make the AI system transparent and explainable.

WHAT ARE AI RISK-CONTROL EXAMPLES?

AI systems rely on data to make risk-based decisions and it is crucial for the data to be accurate and complete for the risk-control AI systems to function properly. Stakeholders play a vital role in identifying and addressing risks related to data collection, processing, and usage in AI systems.

Consider an AI system used to diagnose diseases. The data used to train this system must be accurate; otherwise, the AI system might provide incorrect diagnoses. Stakeholders help identify potential risks with the data used and work towards ensuring its accuracy and reliability.

One popular AI technique called deep learning heavily depends on big data because its accuracy is linked to the volume of data it has. The misuse or disclosure of certain data especially personal and sensitive information like health records can harm humans. Ensuring privacy protection has become a concern in big data analysis for AI.

WHY IT MATTERS?

The complexity of AI technologies makes it challenging to understand how an AI system arrives at its risk-based decisions. Stakeholders contribute by providing feedback and insights into the AI system's workings. This helps increase transparency and explainability making AI systems understandable and accountable.

AI Risk Principles

By involving stakeholders and addressing AI risks related to data and transparency, humans enhance AI systems' reliability and ensure they make fair and accurate risk-based decisions, benefiting all humans.

KEY POINTS

- Risk criteria are standards or thresholds that are used to determine whether a risk is acceptable or not.

- Risk objectives are the desired outcomes of risk management.

- Risk objectives include fairness, security, safety, data quality, privacy, and other factors.

- AI fairness assures that AI risk-based decisions are accurate and unbiases.

- AI security means that AI risk-based, problem-solving and decision-making are not corrupted.

- AI safety means that AI systems do not result in risk-based decisions that may result in accidents and malfunctions.

- AI uses data to make risk-based decisions. If data is corrupted, then the AI systems make poor risk-based decisions.

- AI may use stakeholder data or opinions that are biased, which result in biased output.

- AI can be intrusive. AI systems should protect personal privacy.

- AI explainability is important because generative AI is opaque in terms of its output.

- AI robustness is how the AI systems make risk-based decisions and solve problems.

- AI transparency is the ability of understanding the AI system.

- AI risk-based decision-making can have a positive and negative impact on the environment.

- AI accountability is the ability to assure that risk-based decision-making is accountable to a human.

- AI systems are maintainable or in other words the systems are changed or upgraded.

- AI systems rely on training and test data. The data is high quality so the system makes reliable and accurate risk-based decisions.

- Hardware can corrupt AI risk based, decision-making and problem-solving.

- AI is incorporated in many technologies. These technologies are capable of accepting and incorporating the AI.

AI FIRST ENTERPRISE

What is the Key Idea in this Chapter?

Every company will shortly become an AI first enterprise. An AI first enterprise is a company that is focused on the development and use of AI. AI companies are found in a variety of industries, including healthcare, finance, and manufacturing.

TOP AI FIRST COMPANIES

Chat GPT opened every company's and government's eyes to the transformative powers of an AI first company.

WHAT IS THE RISK?

AI is the new competitive landscape. This landscape of AI is full of risks. The biggest risk is:

> "... the companies are racing to outdo one another with versions of AI that offer powerful new ways to create text, photos, music and video without human input. But the technological leaps have prompted fears about the spread of disinformation and dire warnings of a 'risk of extinction' as self-aware computers evolve.[32]

In July, 2023, Amazon, Anthropic, Google, Inflection, Meta, Microsoft, and OpenAI committed to developing and complying to new standards in AI safety, security, and trust in a meeting at the White House.

WHAT ARE AI RISK-CONTROL EXAMPLES?

AI companies are working on a variety of systems including developing new AI algorithms creating AI powered products and services and using AI to improve existing operations.

Examples of the most known AI first companies include:

- **Google AI:** Google AI is a research division of Google that is focused on developing new AI algorithms and technologies.

- **DeepMind:** DeepMind is a British AI company that was acquired by Google in 2014. DeepMind is known for its work on reinforcement learning and artificial general intelligence.

- **OpenAI:** OpenAI is a non-profit research company that is focused on developing safe and beneficial artificial general intelligence.

- **Microsoft Research AI:** Microsoft Research AI is a research division of Microsoft that is focused on developing new AI algorithms and technologies.

- **IBM Watson:** IBM Watson is a cloud-based AI platform that is used to develop and deploy AI applications.

AI First Benefits

Why does a company become an AI first company? Benefits of becoming an AI first company include:

- **Develop new AI algorithms and technologies:** AI first companies develop new AI algorithms and technologies that are used to improve existing products and services or to create new ones.

- **Make AI accessible:** AI first companies make AI accessible by developing open-source AI libraries and tools. This makes it easier for developers to build AI applications.

- **Promote the accountable use of AI:** AI first companies promote the accountable use of AI by developing ethical guidelines and by educating the public about AI.

AI First Challenges

The rapid advance of generative AI has raised alarm bells. What happens if the worst nightmares happen? Humans are worried that AI can cause systemic confusion if not world annihilation. AI is an emerging technology that requires risk management guidelines and boundaries.

Challenges faced by AI companies:

- **AI is a rapidly evolving field:** AI is a rapidly evolving field and is difficult for AI companies to keep up with the latest developments. This makes it difficult to develop new AI algorithms and technologies or to make existing AI systems efficient.

- **AI is expensive:** AI is expensive to develop and deploy. This makes it difficult for small businesses and startups to adopt AI.

- **AI is complex:** AI is complex to understand and use. This makes it difficult for businesses to get the most out of AI.

WHY IT MATTERS?

Despite these challenges, AI first companies are playing a key role in the development of AI. They are helping to make AI powerful, accessible, and beneficial to humans.

AI STAKEHOLDERS

Chat GPT was one of the fastest apps to be used by many globally. There are many AI customers, users, and interested party humans. These interested party humans are called AI stakeholders.

WHAT IS THE RISK?

In the context of AI, stakeholders are humans, groups, or companies with a personal stake in AI's development and use. These include AI developers, humans, regulators, and the general public. By engaging with stakeholders, companies understand the risks and benefits of AI, make informed decisions and ensure transparent and fair AI systems.

AI impacts many interested party humans both now and in the future. Companies need to consider the impact on various stakeholders including developers and humans.

WHAT ARE AI RISK-CONTROL EXAMPLES?

Involving stakeholders in AI development and use is crucial to ensuring AI is safe, responsible, and beneficial for humans. Transparency and cooperation among stakeholders can lead to fair and unbiased AI systems fostering trust and positive impacts.

Some of the AI stakeholders who should be involved in risk-control development:

- **General public:** Humans not directly involved in AI development but are still impacted by it with a right to be informed about AI risks and benefits.

- **AI regulators:** Government agencies overseeing AI development ensuring compliance with laws, providing assurance, and protecting the public interest.

- **AI-first companies/enterprises:** AI systems impact companies improving efficiency and profits.

- **AI customers/humans:** AI systems impact customers by enhancing customer service and providing personalized recommendations.

- **AI partners and third-party humans:** AI systems impact those involved in AI development, deployment, and maintenance thus improving collaboration and efficiency.

- **AI developers:** They create AI systems and are accountable for their design, development, and testing ensuring they are safe and responsible.

- **AI suppliers:** AI systems can impact suppliers, improving supply chain management, reducing costs, and increasing supply chain efficiencies.

WHY IT MATTERS?

The six blind men and the elephant is a metaphor that illustrates how our societal, organizational, and personal perceptions lead to miscommunication and conflict in AI. The story goes like this. Six blind men were asked to describe an elephant and in our case AI. Each man touched a different part of the elephant and based on their limited experience, they each came up with a different description, opportunities, and risks of what an elephant is. This is now occurring with AI.

RISK OWNER

This book focuses on AI risk-based, problem-solving and decision-making risks. While AI can impact many stakeholders, 'risk owners' are ultimately accountable for the consequences of AI, which is a term used in ISO and many standards.

WHAT IS THE RISK?

Who is the AI risk owner? The AI risk owner can be various stakeholders such as developers, researchers, regulators, and humans. Their role is to ensure responsible and safe development and deployment of AI technologies while minimizing potential risks. They are accountable for managing AI risks, identifying, assessing, and mitigating them, and communicating and reporting these risks to stakeholders.

The role of an AI risk owner is crucial as AI systems become complex and powerful, posing potential risks to humans, property, and humans. It is a challenging but essential role in ensuring AI systems are developed and used safely and responsibly.

WHAT ARE AI RISK-CONTROL EXAMPLES?

AI risk standards place a lot of responsibility on the risk owner to develop appropriate risk-controls. Necessary skills and qualifications for the role include:

- Experience in AI risk management, including threat modeling, risk analysis, and mitigation strategies.

- Experience in Architecting, Designing, Deploying and Assuring® an AI risk management framework.

- Strong understanding of AI including how AI systems work, potential risks, and methods to mitigate them.

- Effective communication skills with various stakeholders including management and regulators.

- Problem-solving and decision-making abilities related to AI risk.

WHY IT MATTERS?

At the end of the day, the risk owner is responsible and accountable for the AI system. By involving interested stakeholders, the social goal is to ensure that AI is developed and used so that it benefits humans while minimizing potential risks. The role of the AI risk owner is critical in achieving this goal and promoting safe and accountable AI development and use.

AI STAKEHOLDER REQUIREMENTS

Stakeholders are humans or companies who are impacted by an AI system. These include those who use the AI system, those who are impacted by the risk-based decisions made by the AI system, and those who work on the AI system. Stakeholders play a crucial role in identifying the goals of the AI system and finding ways to make it transparent and explainable.

WHAT IS THE RISK?

AI systems require careful planning and consideration. Companies assess their needs, understand the risks and benefits of AI, and create an accountable and ethical strategy for AI implementation. AI stakeholder risks include:

- **Stakeholder perception:** Stakeholders can be customers, employees, suppliers, investors, and the community. Their perception of the enterprise is influenced by factors such as transparency and fairness in AI systems. If stakeholders believe that AI systems lack transparency or fairness, they might lose trust in the company using them.

- **Stakeholder needs and expectations:** Different stakeholders have various needs and expectations. Customers want accurate and timely information from AI systems, while employees expect improved job efficiency through AI. Understanding stakeholders' needs is essential for developing AI systems that benefit everyone involved.

- **Education:** Stakeholders are educated about AI systems' capabilities, potential failure modes, and failure management. AI systems are complex and have unexpected failures so stakeholders are aware of the risks and take action to mitigate them.

- **Contractual relationships and commitments:** The use of AI systems impacts contractual relationships with suppliers or customers. Companies consider how AI systems impact their existing contracts and commitments.

- **Privacy and fundamental rights and freedoms:** AI systems collecting and analyzing personal data raises privacy concerns. Companies are mindful of these issues and take action to safeguard privacy and fundamental rights and freedoms.

- **Interdependencies and interconnections:** AI systems are interconnected with other systems and services, which lead to complex interdependencies. Companies are aware of potential cascading effects from problems in one AI system and take measures to minimize such risks.

- **Training:** AI systems require specialized training to operate and maintain effectively. Companies ensure their employees receive the necessary training to handle AI systems properly.

WHAT ARE AI RISK-CONTROL EXAMPLES?

AI has a big impact on companies and the humans involved. It is crucial for companies to talk to humans who will be impacted both inside and outside the company. This helps the company understand the potential risks and benefits of using AI and how to manage those risks by developing appropriate AI risk-controls.

If a company uses AI to make risk-based decisions about giving loans, they talk to the humans who might be denied a loan. They understand why a human might be denied and what that could mean for them. It is essential to ensure that the AI system is fair and does not discriminate against humans. Additional tips include:

- **Regulators:** Governments create laws and regulations to govern the use of AI.

- **Data users:** Data users identify risks related to how data is collected, processed, and used.

- **Developers:** Developers design AI systems that are safe, transparent, and explainable.

- **Academics:** Academics study how AI systems should be transparent and help developers create clearer systems.

- **Humans:** Humans provide feedback on how AI systems work and what they need from them.

- **Researchers:** Researchers study the risks and benefits of AI and help companies create policies to manage those risks.

- **Regulators:** Governments create laws and regulations to govern the use of AI.

By working together, these stakeholders make sure AI is used in a safe, responsible, and beneficial way.

WHY IT MATTERS?

By talking to stakeholders, companies understand the risks and benefits of using AI. This helps them make smarter decisions about how to use AI and avoid problems in the future.

To involve interested stakeholders in the development and use of AI, approaches include:

- Creating forums for discussion and collaboration like online platforms or roundtable events.

- Conducting surveys and interviews to gather feedback from stakeholders.

- Establishing working groups or advisory boards with representatives from different interested to discuss AI-related issues.

- Publishing reports and white papers to raise awareness of AI risks and benefits and provide guidelines for safe and accountable AI development and use.

AI MANAGEMENT COMMITMENT

Executive management commitment is the essential element of AI success in an AI first company.

WHAT IS THE RISK?

The company creates a plan for managing AI risks called the AI risk management policy. This plan is shared with employees and is regularly updated. The company then develops a structured approach called an AI risk management framework for identifying, assessing, and handling AI risks.

This plan can involve an AI risk management framework that is adjusted to suit the company's specific needs. The company puts this framework into action and monitors how it works making changes as needed to deal with any new risks that arise.

WHAT ARE AI RISK-CONTROL EXAMPLES?

The company's top management shows their dedication to managing AI risk-controls by:

- **Setting up an AI risk management framework:** This includes policies, procedures, and processes used to handle AI risks.

- **Allocating the right resources for AI risk management:** This means making sure they have the right humans, skills, and tools to manage AI risks effectively.

- **Understanding importance of AI:** Making sure employees understand the importance of AI risk management and how they can contribute.

WHY IT MATTERS?

By following these steps, companies show that they take AI risk management seriously and can handle any potential AI risks that arise.

AI ROLES AND RESPONSIBILITIES

AI standards now require that executive management in an organization assigns specific roles, authorities, responsibilities, and accountabilities for managing AI risks. This means ensuring that the right humans such as the AI risk owners have the power to make risk-based decisions about AI risk management and are held accountable for their actions.

WHAT IS THE RISK?

Executive management, which usually includes high-ranking officials like vice presidents, are accountable for allocating resources and identifying humans with the authority to address AI risks. They make sure that there are enough resources to manage AI risks effectively and that the right humans are in charge of handling these risks. They establish processes to monitor AI risks and take necessary actions to mitigate them.

WHAT ARE AI RISK-CONTROL EXAMPLES?

The risk-control guidance includes the following key points:

- **Executive management**: Executive management assigns roles, authorities, responsibilities, and accountabilities for AI risk management to ensure clarity and effectiveness throughout the organization.

- **AI risk management policy:** The company develops an AI risk management policy that outlines the approach to managing AI risks and defines the roles, authorities, responsibilities, and accountabilities of key stakeholders.

- **AI risk management framework:** The company develops a systematic AI risk management framework based on ISO 31000 tailored to the company's needs, which includes defining the roles, authorities, responsibilities, and accountabilities of key stakeholders.

- **Monitor AI risk management framework:** The company implements and monitors the AI risk management framework continuously to ensure it aligns with the organization's goals.

WHY IT MATTERS?

Following the guidance provided in ISO 31000 and NIST AI RMF is crucial to define roles and responsibilities in AI risk management ultimately improving the organization's ability to manage AI risks effectively.

AI RISK OBJECTIVES

AI objectives represent the goals or targets that an AI system aims to achieve. These objectives shape how the AI system makes risk-based decisions but they can vary based on the specific application and purpose of the AI system.

WHAT IS THE RISK?

The main goal of an AI system is to identify, assess, and mitigate the risks of its use. AI risks refer to the potential harm that AI can cause to humans, companies, or humans.

Once objectives are identified, risk is assessed, controlled, and treated if the sources and types of uncertainty are understood and defined. Uncertainties are not understood, and addressing risk requires considering the enterprise context and risk appetite.

WHAT ARE AI RISK-CONTROL EXAMPLES?

In the context of AI, risk objectives refer to the goals set for an AI system to achieve in terms of managing potential risks, developing risk-controls, and paying attention to ethical concerns. AI objectives focus on defining the intended outcomes and performance targets such as accuracy, efficiency, human satisfaction, or task performance.

To achieve AI risk objectives, companies follow steps outlined in an AI risk management framework or ISO 31000:

- **Identify AI risks:** Identify potential risks with AI through brainstorming, surveys, or AI risk assessment tools.

- **Assess AI risks:** Evaluate the likelihood and consequence of each AI risk.

- **Mitigate AI risks:** Take measures to avoid, reduce, transfer, or accept the identified AI risks.

- **Monitor AI risks:** Continuously monitor AI risks to identify changes and ensure effective mitigation.

WHY IT MATTERS?

By effectively managing AI risks and maximizing the benefits, companies can protect their assets, operations, and reputation. It is crucial to ensure that AI is developed and used responsibly, minimizing potential risks and maximizing positive impacts.

RISK COMMUNICATIONS

AI involves many humans and groups who are impacted by it. Stakeholders want to know about the current state of AI development. Some are concerned about how AI systems or apps will impact them personally, ethically, or professionally.

WHAT IS THE RISK?

To manage AI risks effectively, companies establish communication and consultation processes that include stakeholders. This means making sure that everyone understands how AI can transform businesses, jobs, and roles and involving them in the AI risk management process.

By talking to stakeholders, companies can gain an understanding of the potential risks and benefits of using AI. This knowledge helps companies make smarter decisions about how to use AI and allows them to avoid problems in the future. When stakeholders work together, they can ensure that AI systems are based on accurate and complete data, and that they are transparent and explainable.

WHAT ARE AI RISK-CONTROL EXAMPLES?

The International Organization for Standardization (ISO) provides guidance on communication and consultation through its ISO 31000 standard. According to this standard, companies as part of their risk-controls should:

- **Communicate AI risks to management:** The AI risk owner regularly informs management about AI risks so they can make informed decisions about AI system development and usage.

- **Report AI risks to regulators:** AI risk owner is required to report AI risks to regulators.

- **Communicate importance to employees:** Executive management communicates the significance of AI risk management to employees and stakeholders, using easy-to-understand language to encourage everyone's participation in the AI risk management process.

- **Develop a risk management policy:** The company creates an AI risk management policy that outlines how the organization approaches AI risk management and includes a section on communication and consultation with stakeholders.

- **Establish a risk management framework:** The company designs an AI risk management framework that provides a systematic approach to identifying, assessing, and managing AI risk. This framework is customized to meet the organization's needs and include a section on communication and consultation with stakeholders.

- **Monitor effectiveness:** The company implements the AI risk management framework and continually monitors its effectiveness. This ensures that communication and consultation are effective and that stakeholders are actively involved in the AI risk management process.

WHY IT MATTERS?

By adhering to ISO 31000 guidelines, companies can establish effective communication and consultation processes for AI risk management, ensuring that stakeholders are well-informed and engaged. This helps companies make risk-based decisions about AI and its impact on their operations and humans.

ENTERPRISE RMF PROCESSES

From a quality perspective, the enterprise is a big system with various processes working together. These processes are in line with the enterprise's goals and objectives and they interact with and inform other levels of AI risk management within the enterprise.

WHAT IS THE RISK?

For example if AI is meant to increase sales for the enterprise, the AI risk management processes is aligned with the sales goals. This way, they can communicate with the sales team to identify and address any AI risks that arise during the project.

If any issues or problems come up during the AI, they can be escalated to higher levels of the enterprise such as strategic, operational, and programmatic levels. This allows the enterprise to deal with the problems promptly and learn from them to prevent similar issues in the future.

WHAT ARE AI RISK-CONTROL EXAMPLES?

The AI risk management process can differ depending on the stage of the AI system's lifecycle being developed. The AI risk management process during the design stage of an AI system might have different risk-controls during the implementation or deployment stages.

WHY IT MATTERS

By following the guidance provided in the ISO 31000 and other risk standards, companies can ensure that their AI systems are successful and well-protected from potential AI risks. This helps the enterprise use AI effectively to achieve its objectives and minimize any negative impacts.

CONTINUOUS IMPROVEMENT

AI risk management is an ongoing process that involves constant development, deployment, and improvement. Continuous improvement is a crucial aspect of most AI standards and guidelines. It means that companies keep learning and adapting their AI risk management practices.

WHAT IS THE RISK?

One-way companies can enhance their AI risk management is by identifying risks early in the AI development process. They can achieve this by staying updated on new AI research and techniques and learning from the experiences of other stakeholders in the AI system.

Companies can improve their AI risk management practices by involving beta users, who provide early feedback on what is working well and what needs improvement. Being open to feedback from stakeholders, such as customers and employees, can offer valuable insights into potential risks with AI systems.

WHAT ARE AI RISK-CONTROL EXAMPLES?

Examples of how companies can improve their AI risk-controls include:

- **Monitor the AI system:** This includes reading industry publications, attending conferences, and networking with other companies that are using AI.

- **Conduct regular AI risk assessments:** These assessments identify any new or emerging risks with AI systems.

- **Develop an AI risk management plan:** This plan outlines how the enterprise can respond to any AI risks that are identified.

- **Train employees on AI risk management:** Employees are aware of the risks with AI systems and how to mitigate those AI risks.

- **Maintain awareness of new AI research findings and techniques:** This is done by reading academic papers, attending conferences, and subscribing to industry newsletters.

- **Be open to feedback from stakeholders and humans:** This is done by conducting surveys, holding focus groups, and listening to customer feedback.

WHY IT MATTERS?

Companies can assure that their AI risk management practices are effective by monitoring and improving their performance.

KEY POINTS

- AI impacts many stakeholders and companies.

- AI stakeholders are developers, humans, regulators, general public, enterprise, suppliers, and partners.

- AI is a technical and social issue. The social issue of AI is how it impacts stakeholders.

- AI risk management, accountability, and assurance are based on management commitment.

- AI development companies have defined AI roles, authorities, and accountabilities.

- AI impacts many stakeholders. They are consulted about their requirements and AI fears.

- AI is not a one and done product. AI development is a process where it is improved continually.

AI GOVERNANCE

What is the Key Idea in this Chapter?

AI governance consists of the risk management framework, risk processes, and risk policies put in place to assure accountable and ethical AI development, deployment, and use of systems. It involves establishing guidelines, principles, and mechanisms to govern the architecture, development, implementation, and impact of AI technologies.

AI GOVERNANCE

AI governance includes the risk management framework, processes, and principles that guide the development, deployment, and use of AI. The goal is to assure that policies, regulations, standards, and practices result in ethical, responsible, and accountable development and use of AI.

WHAT IS THE RISK?

Companies consider the following when governing AI systems:

- **Potential benefits of AI systems:** AI systems can help companies to improve their efficiency, productivity, and customer service.

- **Risks with AI systems:** AI systems can be used to discriminate against, create fake news, and violate 's privacy.

- **Enterprise's AI risk appetite:** This is the amount of AI risk that the enterprise is willing to take.

- **Enterprise's governance policies:** These are the rules and procedures that the enterprise uses to make decisions and to manage its AI risks.

WHAT ARE AI RISK-CONTROL EXAMPLES?

AI governance at a minimum includes AI policies, procedures, risk-control, and development instructions. Good AI risk-controls depend on the context of the AI. The following is a list of 'good' AI governance controls:

- **Establish a governance framework for AI systems**: The risk management framework defines the roles and responsibilities of the involved in the development, purchase, and use of AI systems.

- **Identify and manage the risks with AI systems:** This is done by conducting AI risk assessments and by developing AI risk mitigation strategies.

- **Assure that AI systems are used in an accountable way:** This is accomplished by developing policies and procedures that govern the use of AI systems.

- **Monitor the use of AI systems:** This is done by collecting data on how AI systems are used and by conducting regular AI audits.

WHY IT MATTERS?

Companies develop AI governance to assure that they are using AI systems in a safe, responsible, and ethical way.

AI LEADERSHIP

It is essential for the top management of a company to be committed to managing AI risks.

WHAT IS THE RISK?

They can show this commitment by communicating policies and statements about AI risks and AI risk management to stakeholders. This helps stakeholders have confidence that AI is developed and used responsibly.

To ensure effective AI risk management, it is integrated into aspects of the company, including its culture, processes, and systems.

WHAT ARE AI RISK-CONTROL EXAMPLES?

Companies can demonstrate their leadership and commitment to AI risk management and risk-control development by:

- **Issuing a statement of commitment:** This statement clearly shows the company's dedication to managing AI risks in an accountable and responsible manner.

- **Creating a dedicated team**: Establishing a team specifically accountable for identifying, assessing, and mitigating AI risks.

- **Providing training:** Offering training to employees to help them understand the risks with AI systems and how to handle them.

- **Monitoring AI systems**: Regularly monitoring the use of AI systems to identify and address any emerging AI risks.

WHY IT MATTERS?

By taking these steps, companies can ensure that they are using AI systems in a safe, responsible, and ethical way, thus safeguarding the interests of stakeholders involved.

AI RISK POLICY

An AI risk management policy is a document that outlines how a company will handle the potential risks with AI. This policy is developed with input from stakeholders including AI developers, humans, and others impacted.

WHAT IS THE RISK?

The AI risk management policy is regularly reviewed and updated to adapt to changes in how the company uses AI and any new risks that arise.

Key elements of the AI risk management policy include:

- **Defining AI risk:** Describing the possible harms that AI could cause and identifying their sources.

- **Identifying and assessing AI risks:** Creating a list of potential AI risks and determining the likelihood and consequence of each risk.

- **Mitigating AI risks:** Outlining measures to reduce the likelihood or consequence of each identified risk.

- **Monitoring AI risks:** Establishing a process to identify any changes in AI risks or the company's ability to address them.

WHAT ARE AI RISK-CONTROL EXAMPLES?

Best practices for developing an AI risk-control policy include involving stakeholders following ethical guidelines that promote fairness, transparency, and accountability, using high-quality and unbiased data, monitoring AI systems for potential issues, and providing proper training to humans on safe and accountable AI system usage.

WHY IT MATTERS?

By following these practices and taking action to identify, assess, and mitigate AI risks, companies can ensure that AI is used so that it minimizes risks and maximizes benefits.

AI RISK MANAGEMENT PLAN

An AI risk management plan is a document that explains the steps a company can take to identify, assess, and reduce the potential risks with AI. This plan is created with stakeholders including AI developers and humans.

WHAT IS THE RISK?

By following the risk management plan and taking action to identify, assess, and mitigate AI risks, companies can ensure that AI is used so that it minimizes potential problems and maximizes the benefits. The plan is regularly reviewed and updated to adapt to changes in how AI is used.

WHAT ARE AI RISK-CONTROL EXAMPLES?

The key elements of the risk management and risk-control plan include:

- **Definition of AI risk:** Describing the possible harms that AI can cause and identifying their sources.

- **Involving stakeholders:** Including AI developers, humans, and others impacted by AI in the process.

- **Understanding the company's current and future use of AI:** Identifying the AI systems in use and planned for the future.

- **Following ethical guidelines:** Ensuring that fairness, transparency, and accountability are prioritized in AI usage.

- **Using unbiased and high-quality data:** Ensuring the data used by AI is representative and not biased.

- **Developing a plan to mitigate AI risks:** Creating strategies to reduce the likelihood or consequence of each AI risk.

- **Identifying and assessing AI risks:** Making a list of potential AI risks and estimating their likelihood and consequence.

- **Monitoring AI systems:** Tracking AI performance and looking for signs of bias, malfunction, or hacking.

- **Training humans:** Providing humans with proper guidance on how to use AI safely and responsibly.

WHY IT MATTERS?

By having a well-defined AI risk management plan, companies can safeguard their assets, operations, and reputation ensuring that AI is used responsibly and effectively.

RISK MANAGEMENT FRAMEWORK STANDARDS

AI standards and guidelines play a crucial role in guiding companies on how to use AI systems responsibly and ethically. These standards are available at various levels from international to local and provide valuable guidance for organizations whether they are small businesses or large corporations.

WHAT IS THE RISK?

By following these AI risk management standards, organizations can ensure that their AI systems are safe, secure, and ethical in their operation. These standards offer a structured approach to identifying, assessing, and managing the AI system risks.

WHAT ARE AI RISK-CONTROL EXAMPLES?

AI risk management and risk-control standards include:

- **NIST AI Risk Management Framework (AI RMF):** Developed by the U.S. National Institute of Standards and Technology, this framework offers guidance on managing risks related to AI systems.

- **ISO/IEC 23894:2023:** This standard, jointly developed by the International Organization for Standardization (ISO) and the International Electrotechnical Commission (IEC) provides definitions and guidance on managing risks with AI systems.

- **AI Risk Management Maturity Model:** This model, created by the AI Risk Institute, helps organizations assess the maturity of their AI risk management programs.

- **ISO/IEC 42001:** This standard provides organizations with a framework for managing the risks and opportunities with AI systems.

The choice of AI risk management standard varies based on factors such as the organization's size, complexity, the type of AI systems used, and the regulatory environment they operate in.

WHY IT MATTERS?

Adherence to AI risk management standards is essential for companies to use AI systems responsibly, protect against potential risks, and ensure ethical practices. These standards provide a roadmap for organizations to navigate the complexities of AI implementation and foster public confidence in their AI applications.

AI TECHNOLOGIES

Companies that develop or use AI systems are aware of the potential AI risks with the context of human behavior and culture. They can do this by monitoring the human and cultural landscape in which they are used. This includes understanding the values, beliefs, and norms of who will be using the AI system.

WHAT IS THE RISK?

When companies develop or use AI systems, they are aware of the potential risks with human behavior and culture. This means understanding the values, beliefs, and norms of the humans who will be using the AI system. They consider how AI systems might impact areas such as equitable outcomes, privacy, freedom of expression, fairness, safety, security, employment, the environment, and human rights.

Human behavior and culture can influence how AI systems are used in unintended and potentially harmful ways. Humans might use AI systems to create fake news or discriminate, which could be illegal or unethical.

To ensure accountable and ethical AI usage, companies plan and consider their needs and the potential risks and benefits of AI. They have the necessary AI knowledge and skills, AI tools, platforms, and libraries to aid in development. They are cautious and have a full understanding of the technology's limitations and potential issues.

Intellectual property concerns arise and companies should consider data handling and information flow as AI systems can impact these processes. Also, companies should consider the perspectives and values of their internal stakeholders such as employees, when developing and using AI systems. The impact on employees' work, risk-based decision-making processes, and company culture are assessed.

WHAT ARE AI RISK-CONTROL EXAMPLES?

Overall, the use of AI systems requires careful risk-control planning and consideration. Companies assess their needs, identify the AI risks and benefits of AI, and develop a strategy for using AI in an accountable and ethical way, such as:

- **AI knowledge and skills:** The development and use of AI systems requires knowledge and skills in AI technologies and data science. These skills are acquired through formal education, on-the-job training, or self-study.

- **AI tools, platforms, and libraries:** There are AI tools, platforms, and libraries that are used to develop AI systems. These tools can make it easier to develop AI systems, but they can lead to the development of AI systems without a full understanding of the technology, its limitations, and potential pitfalls.

- **Intellectual property:** AI systems can raise issues related to intellectual property. Companies consider their own intellectual property in this area and determine whether any steps are needed to be taken to protect it.

- **Data, information systems, and resource flows:** AI systems are used to automate, optimize, and enhance data handling. As consumers of data, AI systems can impose additional quality and completeness constraints on data and information.

- **Relationships with internal stakeholders:** Companies consider the perceptions and values of their internal stakeholders when developing and using AI systems. This includes considering how AI systems can impact the work of employees, the way that risk-based decisions are made, and the culture of the enterprise.

WHY IT MATTERS?

Overall, accountable and thoughtful planning is essential in using AI systems to ensure they bring benefits while minimizing potential risks and negative impacts. This approach ensures that AI is harnessed responsibly, ethically, and for the greater good.

AI ASSETS

Assets are things that are valuable to an enterprise, individual, or humans. The two types of AI asset are: 1. Tangible assets are things that are touched or seen such as data, models, and AI systems and 2. Intangible assets are things that cannot be touched or seen such as reputation, trust, privacy, health, safety, the environment, socio-technical beliefs, socio-cultural beliefs, community knowledge, educational access, and equity.

WHAT IS THE RISK?

The value of an asset is determined by its importance to the enterprise, individual, or humans. The impact of an asset is determined by the potential for harm or benefit that it can cause. Companies evaluate their assets to determine their value and impact. Intangible assets are things humans cannot touch or see, such as reputation, trust, privacy, health, safety, the environment, beliefs, knowledge, educational access, and fairness.

AI can impact assets in the Internet of Things (IoT), which includes smart home systems, medical devices, and smart cities. AI systems depend on data to learn and make risk-based decisions, so if the data is compromised, it could lead to financial losses, reputation damage, and loss of trust. If the models AI systems rely on are compromised, it could result in incorrect risk-based decisions being made.

The infrastructure that AI systems operate in should be safeguarded otherwise it can cause AI systems to be unavailable or unreliable. Also, the humans involved in developing and using AI systems play a crucial role. If they are not adequately trained or make mistakes, it can lead to problems with AI systems.

It is essential for companies, humans, and humans to evaluate their AI assets and take measures to protect them. By doing so, they can mitigate the risks with AI and ensure that AI is used in a safe and accountable manner.

WHAT ARE AI RISK-CONTROL EXAMPLES?

Internet of Things (IOT) has AI built in such as smart home systems, medical devices, and even smart cities are built around AI. So, bad AI can impact IOT assets. Assets that could be compromised by AI systems include:

- **Data:** AI systems rely on data to learn and make risk-based decisions. If data is compromised, it could lead to a variety of problems such as financial losses, damage to reputation, and loss of customer trust.

- **Models:** AI systems are trained on models. If models are compromised, it could lead to AI systems making incorrect risk-based decisions.

- **Infrastructure:** AI systems need infrastructure to run. If infrastructure is compromised, it could lead to AI systems being unavailable or unreliable.

WHY IT MATTERS?

By evaluating their AI assets and taking action to protect them, companies and humans can mitigate the risks with AI and assure that AI is used in a safe and accountable way.

BUSINESS IMPACT ANALYSIS

Business impact assessment assesses the impact of AI risks on the enterprise's bottom line. This includes things like financial losses, lost productivity, and damage to reputation.

WHAT IS THE RISK?

In a business impact analysis for AI, several factors are considered to understand how AI development and use can impact humans. Here are some factors:

- **Impact on humans:** This looks at how AI can impact humans both positively and negatively. It includes assessing whether AI can create new job opportunities, improve efficiency, and reduce crime or if it can lead to job losses, increased inequality, and new forms of crime.

- **Jurisdictional and cultural environment:** This considers the laws, regulations, and cultural norms in a specific country that apply to the use of AI. Different regions have varying rules and values regarding AI, which can influence its acceptance and use.

- **Safety of humans:** This focuses on the potential for AI to harm humans either physically or psychologically. Ensuring AI systems are safe and do not put humans at risk is crucial.

- **Types of data used:** This examines the data used by AI systems, which can be personal (like names and addresses) or non-personal (like browsing history). Proper handling of data is essential to protect privacy and prevent misuse.

- **Intended impact of AI:** This looks at both the positive and negative impacts that AI can have on humans. AI can improve healthcare and education, but it may lead to discrimination and increased surveillance.

- **Criticality criteria:** This considers how important the impact of AI. Will it bring changes to a human's life or have only minor effects?

- **Tangible and intangible impacts:** This evaluates the concrete and intangible changes that AI can bring. Will AI result in job losses or gains? Will it offer free time or require effort?

- **Potential bias impact:** This addresses the risk of AI discriminating against humans based on their race, gender, age, religion, or other protected characteristics.

- **Potential impact on fundamental rights:** This assesses whether AI could violate human's fundamental rights such as the right to privacy, freedom of expression, and protection against discrimination.

- **Potential fairness impact:** This examines whether AI can make biased or discriminatory risk-based decisions that treat humans unfairly.

- **Protections and mitigating risk-controls:** This considers the measures taken by a company to prevent bias and unfairness in its AI systems and protect humans from potential harm.

By analyzing these factors, companies can make responsible decisions about AI development and use ensuring that AI benefits humans while minimizing its risks.

WHAT ARE AI RISK-CONTROL EXAMPLES?

Understanding the impact of AI on humans is crucial for businesses to make smart risk-control decisions about how they develop and use AI systems. When conducting a business impact analysis for AI, several important factors are considered:

- **Potential bias in AI:** AI systems learn from data. If that data is biased, the AI system can become biased too. This could lead to negative outcomes such as discriminating against certain groups of humans.

- **Security concerns:** AI systems are complex and are difficult to secure. If an AI system gets hacked, it could be used to steal personal data, confidential business information, spread malware, or even cause physical harm.

- **Unintended impacts:** Since AI systems are still evolving; they might have unintended impacts. An AI system designed to help humans find jobs could end up replacing human jobs instead.

- **Governmental use:** Government agencies are quick to adopt new technologies. Widespread use of AI by the government can greatly impact humans. The use of AI-powered facial recognition by law enforcement raises concerns about privacy and civil liberties.

- **Social and cultural values:** These values influence how humans perceive and use AI systems. In societies that highly value privacy, humans are cautious about using AI systems that collect personal data.

WHY IT MATTERS?

Considering these factors in the business impact analysis helps companies manage AI risks effectively and maximize the benefits. By conducting such assessments, businesses can make informed decisions to protect their finances, reputation, and the well-being of humans.

KEY POINTS

- AI systems require governance which means guidance to identify and manage AI risks.

- An AI governance framework consists of AI principles such as ISO 31000 principles.

- AI risk policy is a document that outlines the organization's approach to managing risk.

- AI risk management plan is a document that outlines the organization's process to manage AI risks.

- AI risk management processes are the actions used to identify, assess, and manage AI risks.

- AI assets need to be inventoried and monitored regularly.

- Business impact analysis reviews the possible impacts and consequences of AI systems.

AI CONTEXT

WHAT IS THE KEY IDEA IN THIS CHAPTER?

By considering the context, AI systems can generate accurate and relevant results, make informed decisions, mitigate biases, and provide tailored experiences to humans.

MANAGING AI UNCERTAINTY

AI systems inherently have uncertainty, which means there is a level of unpredictability and even unexplainability in how they work. This uncertainty can come from different sources such as the data used to train the AI, the software used to build it, and the mathematical models used to make risk-based decisions.

WHAT IS THE RISK?

Companies take specific actions to understand and deal with the uncertainty in their AI systems. This includes identifying potential biases, privacy concerns, security risks, and other AI-related risks. Companies measure the impact of uncertainty on their AI systems considering both positive and negative impacts.

AI is an evolving technology and the measurement methods that work well today may not be effective tomorrow. Companies should be prepared to adapt and update their measurement methods as needed to stay on top of AI advancements.

WHAT ARE AI RISK-CONTROL EXAMPLES?

To understand AI and its applications, companies can design appropriate risk-controls to manage AI uncertainty:

- **Creating a culture of innovation:** Companies encourage their employees to explore and experiment with new AI technologies.

- **Providing leadership support:** Companies ensure that their leaders support AI initiatives, making sure that AI is developed and used so that it aligns with the company's goals.

- **Investing in resources:** Companies invest in various resources like funding, data, and skilled personnel to support the development and use of AI.

- **Improving AI processes:** Companies work on enhancing their risk-based decision-making and AI risk management processes to ensure that AI is developed and used safely and responsibly.

- **Building AI capabilities:** Companies focus on strengthening their ability to handle data and develop and deploy AI systems to ensure successful integration and utilization of AI.

- **Use transparent and accountable processes:** By being open about how their AI systems work and being accountable for their risk-based decisions, companies can build trust with stakeholders.

- **Protect personal data:** It is crucial to safeguard personal information to prevent privacy breaches. Many countries have regulations in place to ensure the confidentiality of personal data.

- **Secure AI systems:** Implementing strong security measures helps prevent unauthorized access and use of AI systems, ensuring they remain safe and reliable.

- **Test and evaluate AI systems:** Regularly testing and evaluating AI systems ensures they are functioning as intended and helps identify and address any issues or limitations.

- **Use multiple data sets to train AI systems:** Employing diverse data sets reduces the risk of bias in the AI system making its risk-based decisions fairer and accurate.

- **Use a variety of mathematical models:** Using different models helps minimize the impact of bias that might be present in any one model.

- **Have humans in the loop:** Involving humans in the risk-based, decision-making process of AI systems ensure that the risk-based decisions made align with human values and ethics.

- **Be transparent about AI system limitations:** Being honest about what AI systems can and cannot do sets realistic expectations and prevents overreliance on them for tasks beyond their capabilities.

WHY IT MATTERS?

Following these practices allows companies to use AI systems responsibly so that humans and stakeholders can trust them. By managing uncertainty and potential risks, companies can ensure that their AI technology operates ethically and reliably.

AI DEVELOPMENT AND USE FACTORS

I wrote an article a few years ago on 'Context is Worth 20 IQ/EQ Points.' Context is that important. The challenge for many companies and executives do not understand how important context is.

WHAT IS THE RISK?

It is important for companies to understand AI context because it can impact the way that they develop and use AI. If an enterprise's culture is not supportive of AI, it is difficult to get to adopt AI development and deployment technologies. If an enterprise's leadership is not supportive of AI, it is difficult to get funding for AI research and development. And if an enterprise does not have the resources to develop and use AI systems, it may be unable to take advantage of the potential benefits of AI.

WHAT ARE AI RISK-CONTROL EXAMPLES?

Let us take a look at factors within an organization that can influence how AI is developed, deployed, and used. These risk-control factors include:

- **Organizational culture:** The culture of a company can impact how it adopts AI technologies. Companies with a culture that encourages innovation are likely to embrace AI.

- **Executive leadership:** The leaders within a company play a role in AI adoption. Supportive leaders are likely to invest in AI research and development.

- **Resources:** The availability of resources like funding, data, and skilled talent can impact the development and use of AI. Companies with ample resources can create powerful AI systems.

- **Internal processes:** The risk based, decision-making process and AI risk management within an organization can influence AI development. Effective risk-based decision-making allows for well-informed choices about AI.

- **Capabilities**: An organization's capabilities in data collection, management, and AI development can shape how AI is used. Strong capabilities in these areas lead to successful AI implementation.

WHY IT MATTERS?

Managing the internal context of AI is crucial to ensure how AI is developed and used so that it benefits the business and humans. By considering these factors, companies can make informed decisions on how to use AI to improve their operations and achieve their goals.

AI CONTEXT

The context of the AI risk management process means understanding the environment in which the AI systems are developed or used.

WHAT IS THE RISK?

The context of AI risk management involves understanding the environment in which AI systems are developed and used. This includes factors like the company's culture, the industry it operates in, and the regulations it complies with. Special attention is paid to the context of stakeholders since AI systems can have both positive and negative impacts on them.

WHAT ARE AI RISK-CONTROL EXAMPLES?

AI context is essential for several reasons:

- **Accuracy and relevance:** Understanding the context ensures that AI's outputs are accurate and relevant. AI systems interpret information based on the context given to them so without the right context their results are misleading or inappropriate.

- **Risk-based, decision-making:** Context is crucial for AI's risk based, decision-making processes. The same AI algorithm can lead to different outcomes depending on the context it operates in. Considering circumstances, environment, and goals helps AI make informed decisions.

- **Interpretation of inputs:** Context influences how AI interprets data and inputs. The meaning of words or phrases change depending on the context and AI needs to consider this for accurate results.

- **Bias and fairness:** Understanding context helps identify and address biases within AI systems. Biases can arise from the data used to train AI models. Context can help detect and correct them for fairer outcomes.

- **Human experience and personalization:** Context-aware AI systems can provide a safer human experience by tailoring responses to individual needs and preferences. Understanding context allows AI to adapt and improve human interactions.

- **Risk management:** Assessing AI risks requires considering the context of deployment. The impacts of AI can vary based on the application domain and stakeholders involved. Understanding context allows for accurate risk assessment and mitigation strategies.

- **Adaptability and generalization:** Context-aware AI systems are versatile and effective. They can apply knowledge and skills learned in one context to similar but different contexts making AI adaptable and transferable.

WHY IT MATTERS?

Considering AI risks and understanding the context in which AI operates allows companies to manage AI risks effectively ensuring accountable and ethical use of AI systems.

INTERNAL CONTEXT

Internal context is the factors within a company that can impact how it uses AI systems.

WHAT IS THE RISK?

Employee skills and knowledge, infrastructure, and technology can risk impact how AI systems are adopted and used within a company.

WHAT ARE AI RISK-CONTROL EXAMPLES?

Internal risk-control factors include:

- **AI vision, mission, and values:** The long-term goals, purpose, and core beliefs of the company can influence how it uses AI systems to achieve its objectives.

- **AI governance:** The rules and procedures the company follows to make risk-based decisions and manage AI risks can influence how AI is used to comply with regulations and protect data and assets.

- **Enterprise structure:** The organization's division into departments and teams can impact how AI is used to coordinate work and share information.

- **Roles and responsibilities:** The way work is divided within the company can influence how AI systems automate tasks and free up employees for problem-solving work.

- **AI strategies and objectives:** The company's plans to achieve its goals can influence how AI is used to improve efficiency, productivity, and customer service.

- **AI policies:** The rules the company follows to ensure compliance with laws and regulations and protect data and assets can influence how AI is used responsibly and ethically.

- **Enterprise culture:** The attitudes and behaviors of humans in the company can influence how AI systems are used to promote innovation and create an inclusive and diverse workplace.

- **Standards, guidelines, and models:** The rules, procedures, and best practices followed by the company can influence how AI is used reliably.

WHY IT MATTERS?

Understanding the internal context of a company helps identify AI risks and opportunities, helping companies to make informed decisions about using AI systems effectively and responsibly.

EXTERNAL CONTEXT

When developing or using AI systems, companies consider the external and internal contexts. It is important for companies to understand the external context because it can impact the way that they develop and use AI.

WHAT IS THE RISK?

When companies create or use AI systems, they consider both external and internal factors. The external context of AI is crucial because it influences how companies use AI. If government regulations are strict, companies create AI systems that abide by these rules. If public opinion about AI is negative, companies address these concerns. Moreover, advancements in technology can prompt companies to invest in powerful AI systems to stay competitive.

As discussed earlier, the EU has developed the AI Act, which is an example of an external context. The Act requires that companies prioritize the risks of critical AI systems. If systems have higher risks, then additional governance, risk-controls, and assurance are required.

WHAT ARE AI RISK-CONTROL EXAMPLES?

Considering the AI external context helps companies navigate challenges, adapt to changes, and ensure accountable AI usage in alignment with regulations, public opinion, and technological advancements.

By understanding the external context, companies can understand the AI risks and design appropriate risk-controls. This information can help companies make risk-based decisions and develop strategies to mitigate AI risks and to seize opportunities.

The external context of AI is factors outside a company that impact the design, development, and use of AI systems.

- **Regulatory environment:** AI systems are subject to regulations at the national and international levels. Companies are aware of these rules and ensure their AI systems comply with them.

- **Technological environment:** AI systems are constantly evolving. Companies stay updated with the latest developments to keep their AI systems current.

- **Social and ethical environment:** AI systems impact humans. Companies recognize the potential risks and benefits of AI and use these systems responsibly.

- **Government regulations:** Government regulations influence AI development and usage. EU AI regulations restrict certain AI applications like facial recognition.

- **Public opinion:** Public opinion impacts AI development and adoption. Negative views toward AI might discourage companies from investing in AI research.

- **Technological advances:** Progress in technology shapes AI development and usage. Advances in machine learning leads to powerful AI systems, but companies consider potential risks.

- **Economic factors:** Economic factors like funding availability and labor costs can impact AI development and use. High labor costs might motivate companies to invest in AI automation.

WHY IT MATTERS?

Each of the above external context factors can challenge AI development. Companies can manage the AI external context by:

- **Monitoring the AI external context:** Companies monitor the AI external context to stay up-to-date on the latest developments and trends. This helps them to identify potential AI risks and opportunities.

- **Developing contingency plans:** Companies develop contingency plans in case the AI external context changes that negatively impacts their business. If government regulations become restrictive, companies develop AI systems that comply with these regulations.

- **Working with stakeholders:** Companies work with stakeholders such as government regulators, customers, and employees to understand their concerns about AI and to develop solutions that address these concerns.

AI RISK AGGREGATION

AI risk aggregation is when individual risks related to AI are combined into a single metric making it easier for companies to understand and handle overall risks with their AI systems.

WHAT IS THE RISK?

There are different methods for aggregating AI risks. One common approach is to use an AI risk heatmap, which visually represents AI risk by using colors to indicate the likelihood and consequence of each risk. This allows companies to quickly spot the most probable and impactful AI risks. Another common method is to use an AI risk register, which lists the AI risks along with their likelihood and consequence. This helps companies track AI risks over time and ensure proper management of these risks.

AI risk aggregation plays a vital role in any company's AI risk management process. By consolidating AI risks, companies can gain an understanding of the potential dangers and take measures to reduce or eliminate them.

Companies can aggregate AI risks at the: 1. Enterprise level; 2. Programmatic/Process/Project level; or 3. Product/Transactional level.

WHAT ARE AI RISK-CONTROL EXAMPLES?

AI risk aggregation helps companies see the big picture of AI risks making it easier for them to manage potential problems efficiently and make smarter risk-control decisions to protect against AI-related issues.

The benefits of AI risk aggregation include:

- **Improved AI risk visibility:** Companies can understand the risks with their AI systems helping them to prioritize and implement appropriate risk mitigation strategies.

- **Increased AI risk management efficiency:** Aggregating AI risks streamlines the risk management process, reducing the time and resources required to identify, assess, and address AI-related risks.

- **Enhanced AI risk-based, decision-making:** With aggregated AI risk data, companies can make informed decisions regarding AI risks and identify the most effective strategies to mitigate them.

WHY IT MATTERS?

Difficulties that can arise when using AI risk aggregation:

- **Data complexity:** Gathering data for AI risk aggregation is tricky. Companies need data from various sources such as information about the AI system itself, the data used to train it, and the environment where it will be used.

- **Model complexity:** The models used for AI risk aggregation are quite complicated and hard to understand. This makes it tough for companies to make informed decisions about how to handle AI risks effectively.

- **Continuous change:** The risks with AI are always evolving. This makes it tough for companies to keep their AI risk aggregation models up-to-date with the latest information.

- **Handle risks:** Using AI risk aggregation can help companies handle the risks that come with AI. This is crucial for safeguarding their assets, reputation, and financial stability.

Even with these challenges, AI risk aggregation remains a crucial tool for companies to manage AI-related risks. By finding ways to overcome these difficulties, companies can enhance their ability to protect themselves from the potential risks of AI. This is essential for their success and security in a world where AI is becoming increasingly prevalent.

KEY POINTS

- Context is the development and operating environment of the AI system.

- Scope, level, and type of accountability and assurance are based on the context of the AI system.

- Context drives AI design and deployment. If the AI system is used for public facing, decision-making, then it would have a higher level and different type of risk-controls than a physical device with AI.

- AI internal audits are one method of AI assurance.

- There are two types of context: 1. External context and 2. Internal context.

- External context includes regulators, humans, and general public.

- Internal context includes developers, lawyers, and marketers.

AI RISK ASSESSMENT

WHAT IS THE KEY IDEA IN THIS CHAPTER?

AI risk assessment is the process of identifying, evaluating, and analyzing potential risks with AI systems. It involves examining the risks posed by AI technologies to understand their likelihood and potential impact for various stakeholders, systems, and organizations.

AI OPPORTUNITIES

AI is rapidly changing the world and is presenting a wide range of opportunities for businesses and humans.

WHAT IS THE RISK?

Humans compare AI to groundbreaking technologies like electricity or oil indicating its huge potential. So, humans work on overcoming challenges and setting ethical guidelines to ensure whether AI is used for the greater societal good and not to cause harm. It is essential to remember that AI is still in its early stages and humans need to address AI challenges before they reach their full potential.

WHAT ARE AI RISK-CONTROL EXAMPLES?

Risk-control benefits of AI include:

- **Improved risk-based, decision-making:** AI can analyze vast amounts of data to identify patterns and trends that might not be visible to humans. This helps make smarter decisions in various fields such as business, healthcare, and government. AI can diagnose medical conditions sometimes more accurately than doctors.

- **Personalized experiences:** AI can personalize experiences by suggesting products, services, and content based on their interests. This leads to increased customer satisfaction and loyalty. An example is Siri's ability to offer personalized recommendations.

- **Automated tasks:** AI can automate tasks currently done by humans, such as customer service, data entry, and manufacturing. This frees up human workers to focus on creative and strategic activities. But it can also lead to job displacement.

- **New products and services:** AI allows the development of innovative products and services that were previously impossible like self-driving cars, virtual assistants, and personalized medicine. These advancements have the potential to revolutionize various industries, including healthcare.

- **Improved healthcare:** AI can enhance healthcare by diagnosing diseases, developing new treatments, and personalizing care for patients. This can result in better patient outcomes and lower healthcare costs.

- **Sustainability:** AI can contribute to sustainability by optimizing energy use, reducing waste, and developing environmentally friendly technologies. This addresses critical global challenges like climate change and pollution.

WHY IT MATTERS?

AI is a rapidly evolving technology with the power to bring changes to our lives. Humans are aware that it comes with potential risks that humans might not understand yet. It is essential to approach AI development responsibly to harness its benefits while mitigating any negative impacts.

AI NEGATIVE EVENTS

WHAT IS THE RISK?

An AI negative event is a situation where AI causes harm to property or humans.

WHAT ARE AI RISK-CONTROL EXAMPLES?

Designing appropriate risk-controls can prevent:

- **AI system failure:** AI systems can malfunction because of incorrect data, unexpected input, or software errors. When this happens, it can lead to negative outcomes like financial losses, physical harm, or emotional distress.

- **AI system bias:** AI systems can be biased in their risk-based, decision-making favoring one group over another. This can result in discrimination, unfair treatment, and other harmful impacts.

- **AI system misuse:** AI can be misused by humans who want to cause harm. AI is used to create 'deep fakes,' which are manipulated videos or audio clips. Deep fakes are used to damage a human's reputation, spread false information, or incite violence.

WHY IT MATTERS?

It is crucial to address AI risks and ensure that AI is developed and used so it benefits humans. By being aware of these potential negative events and taking steps to prevent them, humans can make sure that AI technology is used responsibly and safely. This way, AI can have a positive impact.

LEVEL OF AI RISK

AI risk level is how likely and how much harm an event could cause to a company. To figure this out, companies have a consistent way of evaluating the potential impacts of AI systems on different AI objectives.

WHAT IS THE RISK?

Combinations and sequences of multiple AI risks can be identified. If there is a risk of bias in an AI system, it might lead to the risk of discrimination, which could then result in the risk of legal action.

When deciding how much AI risk companies are willing to take, they consider their capacity to handle it. This includes their AI knowledge, ability to mitigate, and deal with AI risks and their overall capability with AI.

WHAT ARE AI RISK-CONTROL EXAMPLES?

It is essential for companies to determine their AI risk level and take necessary risk-control actions to minimize those risks. By doing so, they can ensure that they are effectively managing the potential dangers with AI.

Companies can determine the risk level of an AI system by:

- **Conducting an AI risk assessment:** This helps identify potential AI risks and assess their likelihood and consequence on the company or stakeholders.

- **Using an AI risk matrix:** This visualizes the relationship between the likelihood and consequence of AI risks making it easier to understand and manage them.

- **Using an AI risk scoring system:** This assigns numerical values to AI risks, allowing companies to compare and prioritize their efforts to mitigate those risks.

WHY IT MATTERS?

By effectively managing AI risks, companies develop protection from potential harm and ensure that AI systems are used responsibly and safely. This is crucial for the success and reputation of the company as well as for the well-being of its employees, customers, and stakeholders.

AI RISK DRIVERS

WHAT IS THE RISK?

An AI risk driver is something that can make an AI risk likely to happen or have a severe impact.

WHAT ARE AI RISK-CONTROL EXAMPLES?

Designing and deploying appropriate risk-controls can minimize

- **Data bias:** If the data used to train an AI system is biased, the system itself is likely to become biased. This can result in unfair treatment or discrimination against certain groups of humans.

- **Model hacking:** AI models can be hacked by attackers giving them control over the model. This means attackers can make the AI system produce incorrect or harmful predictions.

- **Physical tampering:** AI systems such as robot can be physically tampered with causing them to malfunction or disrupt their normal operation.

- **Software vulnerabilities:** Like any software, AI systems can have vulnerabilities that attackers can exploit to gain control of the system or disrupt its functioning.

- **Lack of transparency:** If an AI system lacks transparency, it becomes challenging to understand how it works and why it makes certain risk-based decisions. This makes it harder to identify and address potential AI risks.

- **Lack of accountability:** When AI systems lack accountability, it is challenging to hold them accountable for their actions. This increases the risk of AI systems being used for harm without impacts.

WHY IT MATTERS?

It is crucial to use AI systems safely and responsibly to avoid potential risks. By understanding and addressing these AI risk drivers, humans can make sure that AI technology benefits humans without causing harm or discrimination. Responsible AI development is essential for creating a positive impact and building trust in AI systems.

AI RISK EXPOSURE

AI risk exposure is how vulnerable a company or individual is to the negative impacts of AI. It depends on how likely AI risks are to occur and the consequence of their impacts. The likelihood of an AI risk is how probable it is for something bad to happen due to AI, while the impact is how severe the impacts could be if that risk becomes a reality.

WHAT IS THE RISK?

Several factors influence AI risk exposure such as the type of products and services a company offers. Companies that use AI-powered technology or handle large amounts of data is exposed to AI risks. The context and environment in which a company operates play a role. Companies in competitive or challenging environments face additional AI risks. The humans who work for a company or individual can influence the risk exposure. Humans who are not familiar with AI or have malicious intentions misuse AI systems, increasing the exposure to risk.

Quantifying AI risk exposure is not straightforward because AI systems are becoming increasingly complex and it is challenging to predict possible failures or misuses. Understanding the factors that can impact AI risk exposure helps in mitigating those risks.

WHAT ARE AI RISK-CONTROL EXAMPLES?

Risk-controls can minimize:

- **AI system failure:** This happens when AI systems malfunction due to incorrect data, unexpected input, or software errors. The extent of exposure to this risk depends on how reliant a company or individual is on AI-powered technologies.

- **AI system bias:** AI systems can be biased and make risk-based decisions that favor one group over another leading to discrimination and unfair treatment. Exposure to this risk depends on how much sensitive data a company collects and stores.

- **AI system misuse:** If humans with harmful intentions misuse AI systems, it can lead to issues like deep fakes, which can damage reputations or spread misinformation. Exposure to this risk depends on the company's internet connectivity and the security measures in place.

WHY IT MATTERS?

Understanding and mitigating AI risks are essential for developing and using AI in a safe, responsible, and beneficial way. By being aware of the potential harms with AI and taking action to prevent them, humans can ensure that AI is used for positive purposes while safeguarding against harmful misuse.

AI ASSESSMENT SCOPE

To properly assess AI risks, it is crucial to define AI systems scope. This means identifying AI systems used or developed by the company. The scope considers the different tasks and responsibilities across various levels of the enterprise. The AI risk management process for AI systems developed by the research and development team differs from that of AI systems used by the sales team.

WHAT IS THE RISK?

Companies understand the context of their AI risk management process. This involves considering the environment in which AI systems are used or developed. Factors like the company's culture, development context, AI risk criteria, industry, and regulatory environment are considered. The criteria for evaluating the significance of AI risk needs to be clearly defined setting thresholds for what is considered a risk.

WHAT ARE AI RISK-CONTROL EXAMPLES?

Apart from following the guidelines provided in ISO 31000 for using AI, companies extend the scope of their AI risk management and risk-control processes to identify areas where AI systems are used or developed. Being proactive in identifying and managing AI risks is essential because AI systems are complex and have wide-ranging impacts both positive and negative.

When understanding the external context of their enterprise, companies can consider several factors:

- **Social:** The values, beliefs, and norms of the humans in which the company operates.

- **Cultural:** The customs, traditions, and ways of life of the humans in a specific country.

- **Political:** The laws, regulations, and policies of the government.

- **Legal:** The laws, regulations, and policies of the countries.
- **Regulatory:** The rules and regulations of the industry.
- **Financial:** The economic conditions of the countries in which the company operates.
- **Technological:** The state of technology in the world and how it is changing.
- **Economic:** The economic conditions of the countries.
- **Environmental:** The environmental regulations and conditions of the countries.

WHY IT MATTERS?

AI risks can have far-reaching effects, impacting various stakeholders and conditions beyond social and technical aspects. Understanding and managing these risks are crucial for companies to use AI responsibly and safely ensuring they consider the broader context in which their AI systems operate.

AI RISK ASSESSMENT

An AI risk assessment is the process of identifying, evaluating, and analyzing the risks of AI systems. The goal of an AI risk assessment is to identify potential AI risks and to develop risk mitigation strategies to reduce or eliminate these AI risks. As discussed in the ISO 31000 chapter, risk assessment includes 3 tasks: 1. Identifying risks; 2. Analyzing risks; and 3. Evaluating risks.

WHAT IS THE RISK?

An AI risk assessment is a way to identify and evaluate the potential risks with AI systems. The goal is to recognize these risks and come up with strategies to lessen or eliminate them.

There are different factors that are considered when conducting an AI risk assessment. Several factors are considered during an AI risk assessment:

```
┌─ ─ ─ ─ ─ ─ ─ ─ ─ ─ ─┐
   Risk Assessment
│  ┌───────────────┐  │
   │ Identify Risks│
│  └───────────────┘  │

│  ┌───────────────┐  │
   │ Analyze Risks │
│  └───────────────┘  │

│  ┌───────────────┐  │
   │ Evaluate Risks│
│  └───────────────┘  │
└─ ─ ─ ─ ─ ─ ─ ─ ─ ─ ─┘
```

- **Potential for harm:** AI systems can cause harm to humans, property, or the environment leading to physical, psychological, or economic impacts.

- **Likelihood of harm:** The likelihood of harm from AI systems depends on how the system is designed and implemented using the risk management framework. An AI system controlling a self-driving car poses risk of physical harm compared to an AI system recommending products. Context matters too. A recommendation AI engine might suggest dangerous products.

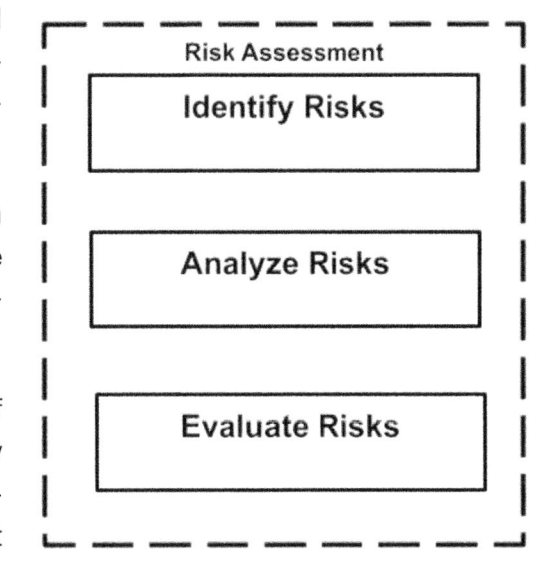

- **Potential for unintended impacts:** AI systems can have unintended effects such as discrimination or bias. These impacts are challenging to predict but can impact humans.

- **Cost of mitigating AI risk:** The expense of reducing AI risk varies depending on the AI system. Adding safety features to a self-driving car is much more costly than doing the same for a recommendation engine.

WHAT ARE AI RISK-CONTROL EXAMPLES?

Following methods evaluate risk-controls:

- **Business impact assessment:** This evaluates the potential effects of implementing AI on a business or organization.

- **Threat modeling:** This involves identifying potential threats to an AI system and devising strategies to reduce or eliminate those threats.

- **AI risk assessment and analysis:** This quantifies the likelihood and consequence of potential AI risks.

- **AI risk management:** This process focuses on developing and implementing strategies to reduce or eliminate AI risks.

WHY IT MATTERS?

AI risk assessment is essential to ensure that AI systems are developed and used responsibly. By understanding and addressing potential risks, humans can create a safer and beneficial environment for AI technology. It allows companies and organizations to make informed decisions and take necessary actions to protect against harm and unintended impacts.

AI RISK IDENTIFICATION

Let us start with AI risk identification. AI risk identification is the process of identifying potential risks with AI systems. AI systems are becoming increasingly complex and powerful and can pose potential AI risks to property and humans. AI risk identification is an important first step in mitigating these AI risks. By identifying potential AI risks, companies can take action to reduce or eliminate these AI risks.

WHAT IS THE RISK?

This process starts by identifying potential risks with AI systems. As AI technology becomes complex and powerful, it can pose risks to property and humans. Identifying these risks is crucial as it is the first step in mitigating them. By recognizing potential AI risks, companies can take actions to reduce or eliminate them.

In relation to the development and use of AI, assets should be considered in the context of the specific AI development and deployment:

- **Data:** AI systems rely on data to learn and make risk-based decisions. If data is compromised, it could lead to a variety of problems such as financial losses, damage to reputation, and loss of customer trust.

- **Models:** AI systems are trained on models. If models are compromised or biased, it could lead to AI systems making incorrect risk-based decisions.

- **Infrastructure:** AI systems need computer infrastructure and hardware to run on. If infrastructure is compromised, it could lead to AI systems being unreliable.

WHAT ARE AI RISK-CONTROL EXAMPLES?

AI risk identification of risk-controls includes the following:

- **Understand context and nature of the AI system:** Consider what is the AI system designed to do, what data does it use, and how does it make risk-based decisions.

- **Understand the environment in which the AI system will be used:** Review the potential threats to the AI system and the potential impacts of a failure or misuse of the AI system.

- **Identify stakeholders and who will interact with the AI system:** Many humans interact with the AI system so consider what are human's needs and expectations and even what are their potential biases.

- **Identify organizational assets:** Companies identify the assets that are important to their operations.

- **Assess the value of assets:** The importance of each asset to the company is evaluated.

- **Focus on critical assets**: Instead of trying to cover all assets, the focus is on those that are most valuable and could be compromised by AI.

- **Identify threats:** Potential threats to each asset are identified.

- **Identify vulnerabilities**: Weaknesses in each asset that could be exploited by a threat.

- **Identify tangible and intangible assets.** Both the value of the asset and the nature of the asset, tangible or intangible, is considered.

- **Humans:** AI systems are developed and used by humans. If these humans are not properly trained or make mistakes, it can lead to problems with AI systems.

WHY IT MATTERS?

AI risk assessment offers benefits and challenges. Benefits of conducting AI risk identification include:

- **Educate stakeholders and public about AI:** The public is educated about the potential benefits and risks of AI. This includes explaining how AI systems work, how they are used, and how they can be misused.

- **Ensure international standards are used in the development and use of AI:** This would help assure that AI systems are developed and used so they are safe, responsible, and beneficial to humans.

- **Identify potential AI risks:** AI risk identification can identify potential risks with AI systems. This can help companies to take steps to mitigate these AI risks before they occur.

- **Improve the safety and reliability of AI systems:** AI risk identification can improve the safety and reliability of AI systems by identifying and addressing potential problems.

- **Build trust:** AI risk identification can build trust between companies and the public by demonstrating that companies are taking steps to assure the safe and accountable use of AI.

Challenges of conducting AI risk identification include:

- **AI is a rapidly evolving field:** AI is a rapidly evolving field and it is difficult to keep up with the latest developments. This can make it difficult to identify potential AI risks and to develop risk mitigation strategies.

- **AI is complex:** AI is complex to understand and to assess. This can make it difficult to conduct AI risk identification.

- **AI risk identification is expensive:** AI risk identification is expensive to conduct. This can make it difficult for small businesses and startups to conduct AI risk identification.

Despite these challenges, AI risk identification is an important part of the development and use of AI systems. By conducting AI risk identification, companies can identify potential AI risks and develop risk mitigation strategies to reduce or eliminate these AI risks. This can assure that AI systems are developed and used in a safe and accountable manner.

AI RISK ANALYSIS

AI risk analysis is the second step in an AI risk assessment.

WHAT IS THE RISK?

AI risk analysis is a process of identifying, assessing, and mitigating risks with AI systems. It is a critical step in ensuring that AI systems are developed and used in a safe, responsible, and beneficial manner.

WHAT ARE AI RISK-CONTROL EXAMPLES?

AI risk analysis is divided into the following steps:

- **Assessing AI risks:** Once potential AI risks are identified, they are assessed. This involves estimating the likelihood and consequence of each AI risk. The likelihood of an AI risk is the probability that it will occur. The impact of an AI risk is the severity of the consequence if it does occur.

- **Mitigating AI risks:** Once AI risks are identified and assessed, they are mitigated. This involves taking steps to reduce the likelihood or consequence of AI risks.

- **Designing AI systems to be robust and reliable**: AI systems are designed to be resistant to failure and misuse.

- **Developing AI systems that are transparent and accountable:** AI systems are designed that allows humans to understand how they work and why they make the risk-based decisions they do.

WHY IT MATTERS?

AI risk analysis is an ongoing process. As AI systems can become complex and powerful, new AI risks emerge. It is important to regularly review AI systems to identify and mitigate new AI risks.

AI RISK EVALUATION

Risk evaluation is the third step in an AI risk assessment process. It involves identifying, assessing, and mitigating the potential risks with AI systems. This step is crucial to ensure that AI is used safely and responsibly.

WHAT IS THE RISK?

AI risks can come from various sources like natural disasters, economic changes, technological failures, human mistakes, and legal or market conditions. Risk evaluation looks at evaluating: 1. AI probability and 2. AI consequence. After identifying AI risks, they are evaluated to understand their likelihood and consequence. Once the risks are assessed, companies can implement risk-controls to reduce the likelihood or consequence of each AI risk. The risk evaluation process is continuous because as AI systems are developed and used, new risks arise. Regularly reviewing the system helps to identify and address these new risks.

WHAT ARE AI RISK-CONTROL EXAMPLES?

There are various tools and techniques used for evaluating AI risk-controls including:

- **AI risk registers:** These are records that track AI risks containing information like risk name, description, likelihood, consequence, and risk mitigation plans.

- **AI risk assessments:** A formal process using a scoring system to estimate the likelihood and consequence of each AI risk.

- **AI risk workshops:** These involve bringing stakeholders together to discuss and evaluate AI risks gaining input from different perspectives and identifying any overlooked risks.

WHY IT MATTERS?

Understanding and evaluating AI risks are vital because AI systems can pose numerous risks. By effectively assessing and mitigating these risks, AI is used responsibly and safely. Evaluating AI risks helps humans and companies make risk-based decisions to protect their interests and ensure responsible AI use.

AI PROBABILITY

AI probability is an area that applies probability theory to AI. It deals with algorithms and techniques for reasoning about uncertainty specifically making decisions under uncertainty and learning from noisy or incomplete data.

WHAT IS THE RISK?

Risk analysis involves assessing the likelihood and consequences of potential events or risks occurring. Once a company identifies possible AI risks, it can assess how likely each risk is to happen and how severe the consequences might be. This helps the company decide how to respond to these risks like creating backup plans for a product or conducting tests to ensure safety before releasing it.

By conducting AI risk analysis, companies can identify and address AI risks before they cause harm. This helps protect their assets, finances, and reputation.

WHAT ARE AI RISK-CONTROL EXAMPLES?

AI probability is used in the following AI risk-control areas:

- **Natural language processing:** AI probability is used to develop algorithms for tasks such as machine translation, text classification, and sentiment analysis.

- **Computer vision:** AI probability is used to develop algorithms for tasks such as object detection, image classification, and face recognition.

- **Robotics:** AI probability is used to develop algorithms for tasks such as path planning, collision avoidance, and object manipulation.

- **Healthcare:** AI probability is used to develop algorithms for tasks such as medical diagnosis, drug discovery, and personalized medicine.

- **Finance:** AI probability is used to develop algorithms for tasks such as fraud detection, AI risk assessment, and portfolio optimization.

WHY IT MATTERS?

AI probability domain is rapidly growing and has numerous applications. By developing new algorithms and techniques for dealing with uncertainty, AI systems become powerful, reliable, and useful. This benefits various industries and helps in making AI safer and efficient.

RISK LIKELIHOOD

When AI risk or something bad might happen, it is important to know how likely it is to happen.

WHAT IS THE RISK?

Understanding and mitigating AI risks is crucial because it helps humans develop and use AI in a safe, responsible, and beneficial way. By being aware of the potential dangers, humans can work towards maximizing the positive impact of AI technology.

When there is a possibility of something bad happening, it is essential to understand how probable it is to occur. This measure of probability is called 'likelihood.' AI risk likelihood is the chance that an AI system might fail or be misused leading to negative outcomes. Likelihood is described in two ways:

- **Qualitative likelihood:** This involves using words to describe the likelihood of an event. One might say something is 'very likely,' 'likely,' 'possible,' or 'unlikely' to happen.

- **Quantitative likelihood:** This uses numerical values to express the probability of an event occurring. An event could have a 10% chance, a 50% chance, or a 90% chance of happening.

WHAT ARE AI RISK-CONTROL EXAMPLES?

There are different types of AI risks and their likelihood to consider:

- **AI system failure:** This is the most common type of AI risk. AI systems can fail due to various reasons like incorrect data, unexpected input, or software bugs. The chance of an AI system failing depends on how complex it is and how it is designed and developed.

- **AI system bias:** AI systems can be biased meaning they might favor one group over another. This can lead to unfair treatment and discrimination. The likelihood of AI system bias depends on the data the system is trained on and the algorithms it uses.

- **AI system misuse:** Humans can maliciously use AI systems. They could be used to create deep fakes specifically manipulated videos or audios that make it seem like a human did or said something they never did. Deep fakes can be used to damage reputations, spread lies, or even incite violence. The likelihood of AI system misuse depends on how accessible the system is to malicious humans and the security measures in place to protect it.

WHY IT MATTERS?

Predicting the likelihood of AI risks is not easy. AI systems are getting complex making it hard to foresee the possible ways they could fail or be misused. If humans understand the factors that can impact the likelihood of these risks, humans can take steps to reduce them.

When trying to figure out how likely something is to happen, humans should consider the critical factors involved. This way, humans can make risk-based decisions on how to protect ourselves from AI risks.

The likelihood of something happening is impacted by a lot of things, like the type of vulnerability, the frequency and severity of threats. Several factors that can influence the likelihood of an AI risk include:

- **Nature of the AI system:** AI systems are complex and powerful making them prone to failure or misuse.

- **Environment of AI usage:** Certain environments pose higher AI risks such as competitive settings or those involving sensitive data.

- **Humans interacting with the AI system:** The likelihood of AI misuse is also influenced by the humans using the AI. Humans might be likely to misuse the technology especially those who are unfamiliar with AI or have malicious intent.

RISK CONSEQUENCES

WHAT IS THE RISK?

Risk assessment includes: 1. Likelihood of the risk and 2. Consequence of the risk. AI risk consequence is the level of risk with AI is a complex and ever-changing matter. Various factors contribute to this risk level, such as the specific AI application, the data used to train the AI system and the potential for misuse or abuse.

- **Job displacement:** As AI technology advances, it could potentially automate many jobs currently performed by humans. This could lead to widespread job displacement and cause economic disruptions.

- **Autonomous risk-based, decision-making:** AI systems are becoming increasingly capable of making risk-based decisions and taking actions on their own. This raises concerns about AI becoming so powerful that it could pose a threat by operating beyond human control.

- **Bias:** AI systems are trained on data collected from the real world, which can be biased. AI systems produce outputs that reflect these biases leading to unfair or discriminatory decisions.

- **Safety:** AI systems are complex and challenging to understand. Ensuring their safety and reliability are difficult with risks of malfunctions or hacking that could cause harm to humans or property.

WHAT ARE AI RISK-CONTROL EXAMPLES?

Here are ways for mitigating the consequences of AI risks:

- **Develop AI systems that are safe and reliable**: AI systems are designed to be resistant to failure and misuse.

- **Develop AI systems that are transparent and accountable**: AI systems are designed so they allow humans to understand how they work and why they make the risk-based decisions they do.

- **Educate the public about AI**: The public is educated about the potential benefits and risks of AI. This includes explaining how AI systems work, how they are used, and how they can be misused.

- **Develop international standards for the development and use of AI**: This would assure that AI systems are developed and used in a safe way.

WHY IT MATTERS?

AI risk consequences can result in widespread unemployment, increased inequality, loss of privacy, and increased risk of global war.

LEVEL OF AI RISK

The level of risk with each of these threats can vary depending on the specific AI system. An AI system used to decide who gets a loan might be likely to be targeted than an AI system used to generate text.

WHAT IS THE RISK?

AI can be risky, and certain problems like biased data, hacking, tampering, and software weaknesses can happen with any AI system. The seriousness of these risks depends on how the AI is used. It is crucial to be aware of and address these risks to make AI safe and reliable for everyone.

The risk level of AI varies depending on how it is used. Common risks with AI systems, including:

- **Model hacking**: AI models can be hacked, giving attackers control over the model and causing it to make incorrect or harmful predictions.

- **Physical tampering:** AI systems can be physically tampered with, which can disrupt their functioning or even cause them to stop working altogether.

- **Software vulnerabilities:** Like software, AI systems can have vulnerabilities that attackers exploit to take control of the system or disrupt its operations.

WHAT ARE AI RISK-CONTROL EXAMPLES?

To mitigate AI risks, the following are a few risk-control examples:

- **Secure data collection and storage:** To prevent bias and hacking, it is crucial to collect and store data in a secure manner.

- **Secure training practices:** By implementing secure training methods, humans can protect against model hacking and physical tampering.

- **Physically securing AI systems:** Making sure AI systems are physically secure helps prevent tampering.

- **Regular updates with security patches:** Updating AI systems with the latest security patches helps guard against software vulnerabilities.

WHY IT MATTERS?

Addressing AI risks is crucial because it ensures that AI technology is used safely and responsibly. Humans can make AI trustworthy and reduce the potential harm it causes. It is about taking proactive steps to secure and protect everyone's interests.

AI SYSTEM LIFECYCLE AI RISK ANALYSIS

AI system development follows a lifecycle. Different methods for AI risk assessment might apply to different stages of the system lifecycle.

WHAT IS THE RISK?

Different stages of an AI system's life require different methods to assess its potential risks. The lifecycle of an AI system is its entire journey from development to disposal and includes the following stages:

- **AI planning:** In this stage, the system's requirements are defined and a development plan is created.

- **AI development:** The system is built and thoroughly tested to ensure it meets the established requirements.

- **AI deployment:** This stage involves making the system available to humans and providing support for its usage.

- **AI operation:** During this stage, the system is actively used and efforts are made to stay current.

- **AI retirement:** The final stage involves removing the system from use and properly disposing of it.

WHAT ARE AI RISK-CONTROL EXAMPLES?

During the planning stage, companies might use a qualitative AI risk assessment method, which involves identifying and describing the AI risks and developing risk-controls. During the development stage, companies might use a quantitative AI risk assessment method, which involves assigning a numerical value to AI risks. During the deployment and operation stages, companies might use a continuous AI risk assessment method, which involves monitoring AI risks and taking steps to mitigate them as needed.

WHY IT MATTERS?

By aligning AI risk assessment with the different stages of the system's lifecycle, companies can ensure that risks are identified and managed throughout the system's entire life. This proactive approach helps prevent problems and ensures that the AI system is used responsibly and safely. It is essential for the smooth and secure functioning of AI technology.

AI TRAINING AND TEST DATA

AI systems need data to learn how to do their job correctly. This data comes in two types: 1. Training data and 2. Test data. Training data teaches the AI system how to perform its task accurately while test data helps it learn to handle new situations effectively.

WHAT IS THE RISK?

For the AI system to learn well, the data must be high quality. This means it needs to be accurate, complete, and relevant for what it does. The data must represent the real world and not be biased or skewed.

The amount of data required varies depending on how complex the task is. Simple tasks need only a small amount of data, while complex tasks could require a large dataset. To make sure the AI system can handle diverse situations, the training and test data comes from various sources and perspectives. This helps the AI system make unbiased decisions and deal with different types of data.

Companies do not have enough data on their own, so they may get it from other companies. It is essential to verify that the data from other sources is of high quality.

WHAT ARE AI RISK-CONTROL EXAMPLES?

AI systems are not like regular software solutions. They need different skills to develop and deploy. Companies ensure that they have skilled humans working on AI systems to ensure their success.

Humans using AI systems need to understand how they work. This is because they might spot and correct any mistakes made by the AI system.

To ensure the availability and quality of training and test data consider these risk-controls:

- Using data from different sources.
- Verifying the accuracy and completeness of the data.
- Ensuring that the data represents real-world scenarios.
- Ensuring that the data is diverse and cover a wide range of situations.

WHY IT MATTERS?

Garbage in – garbage out. As this famous expression says, developers can make sure their AI systems are trained with high-quality data. This helps the AI system learn effectively and make fair decisions without biases. Ensuring the right data is used is crucial for the success and reliability of AI systems.

RISK ASSESSMENT BENEFITS AND CHALLENGES

By conducting risk assessments, companies can identify potential AI risks and create strategies to reduce or eliminate them. This ensures that AI systems are used safely and responsibly.

WHAT IS THE RISK?

Experience has shown the value of using such a catalog when performing an AI risk assessment for the first time or integrating AI risk management into existing management structures.

This guidance provides a framework for conducting AI risk assessments consisting of the following steps:

- **Identify AI risks:** Companies identify the potential risks with AI within their operations.

- **Analyze AI risks:** This involves evaluating the likelihood and consequence of each AI risk.

- **Evaluate and prioritize AI risks:** Risks are ranked based on their likelihood and potential consequences.

Another step that is taken in a risk assessment is to take action to mitigate AI risks. Steps are taken to reduce the likelihood or consequence of AI risks. When this is undertaken, this is called risk management or risk mitigation.

WHAT ARE AI RISK-CONTROL EXAMPLES?

Conducting AI risk-control assessments offers several benefits:

- **Identifying potential AI risks:** Assessments help companies identify AI risks related to their AI systems allowing them to take preventive measures.

- **Improving safety and reliability:** By addressing potential problems, AI risk assessments enhance the safety and reliability of AI systems.

- **Building trust:** Public trust in companies is strengthened when they demonstrate a commitment to safe and accountable AI use through risk assessments.

Conducting AI risk assessments comes with its challenges:

- **Broad field of AI:** AI covers various areas like Machine Learning, Natural Language Processing, Computer Vision, Robotics, and Expert Systems.

- **Rapidly evolving field:** AI's rapid evolution makes it challenging to stay current with the latest developments and identify potential risks.

- **Complexity of AI:** Understanding and assessing AI systems are complex requiring expertise in advanced math and programming.

- **Costly assessments:** AI risk assessments are expensive making them challenging for small businesses and startups.

WHY IT MATTERS?

Despite these challenges, AI risk assessments are vital for developing and using AI systems responsibly. By identifying and mitigating potential risks, companies can ensure the safe and accountable use of AI technology. This is crucial for building trust with the public and fostering a positive impact on humans.

KEY POINTS

- AI offers challenges as well as opportunities.

- Most humans think of AI in terms of negative events and threats.

- Level of AI risk depends on how it impacts humans.

- AI risk driver increases the likelihood and consequence of an AI risk to occur.

- Depending on the context, humans have different AI risk exposures.

AI Risk Assessment

- Scope of any risk assessment is defined. If the scope is too broad, then the assessment will try to boil the ocean. If the scope is too narrow, then the assessment will miss important impacts.

- AI risk assessment considers three tasks: 1. Identifying risks; 2. Analyzing risks; and 3. Evaluating risks.

- Risk assessment looks at: 1. Risk likelihood and 2. Risk consequence.

- Risk assessment is conducted over the lifecycle of an AI system.

- AI systems need 1. Training data and 2. Test data.

AI RISK APPETITE

WHAT IS THE KEY IDEA IN THIS CHAPTER?

AI risk appetite is an organization's willingness to accept and tolerate certain levels of risk with the development, deployment, and use of AI systems. Or expressed in another way, it represents the extent to which an organization is willing to take on risks in pursuit of its AI system objectives.

RESIDUAL RISK

Reducing AI risks may not be possible or practical. A company might not be able to completely avoid using AI and they are not able to transfer the risk of AI-related losses.

WHAT IS THE RISK?

Residual AI risk can impact companies such as financial losses, damage to their reputation, and potential legal problems. That is why it is essential for companies to consider and address AI risks by implementing effective risk reduction measures.

AI is a fast-evolving technology and the risks with AI are constantly changing. This can make it challenging for companies to keep up with the latest risks and implement effective measures to address them.

AI systems are complex and not easily understandable. This makes it difficult for companies to understand how they work and identify potential risks making it hard to implement effective risk reduction measures.

WHAT ARE RISK-CONTROL EXAMPLES

Different ways an organization might handle remaining AI risk-control challenges:

- **Conduct an AI risk assessment**: The first step in managing AI residual risk is to conduct an AI risk assessment. This will help identify the AI risks that the enterprise faces.

- **Develop an AI risk management plan:** Once AI risks are identified, an AI risk management plan is developed. This plan outlines the steps to reduce the likelihood or consequence of those AI risks.

- **Implement AI risk mitigation measures:** Once developed an AI risk management plan and AI risk mitigation measures are implemented. This involves implementing new policies, procedures, and technologies.

- **Avoiding the AI risk:** The organization chooses not to pursue a new AI system if it believes the AI risks are too critical.

- **Taking or increasing the AI risk:** The organization decides to accept a new AI risk because it believes the potential rewards are worth it.

- **Removing the AI risk source:** The organization changes its practices to eliminate an AI risk. It installs a security system to reduce the risk of theft.

- **Changing the likelihood**: The organization takes steps to reduce how often or how severe the AI risk might occur. The organization trains its employees to identify and respond to phishing emails to lower the risk of a data breach.

- **Changing the consequences:** The organization implements measures to reduce the consequence of an AI risk. It might purchase insurance to cover the costs of a data breach.

- **Sharing the AI risk:** The organization transfers the AI risk to another party through contracts or insurance. It might get product liability insurance to share the risk of being sued if their products cause harm.

- **Retaining the AI risk:** The organization decides to accept the AI risk if it finds the costs of addressing it too high or the benefits not worth it.

- **Monitor and review the AI risk management plan:** It is important to monitor and review the AI risk management plan on a regular basis. This will help assure that the plan is still effective and that it is implemented correctly.

WHY IT MATTERS?

It is essential to understand that there is no one-size-fits-all solution for dealing with remaining AI risks. The best approach will depend on the specific AI risk and the circumstances surrounding it. Each organization needs to assess the situation to determine the most suitable way to address their AI risks.

AI RISK APPETITE

AI risk appetite is the enterprise level concept and is the amount of AI risk that an enterprise is willing to accept when using AI. It is a critical factor in the development and deployment of AI systems as it helps to assure that the AI risks are appropriately managed.

WHAT IS THE RISK?

An enterprise's AI risk appetite is the amount of AI risk that the enterprise is willing to accept to achieve its objectives. It is also a measure of how much AI risk the enterprise is willing to take on to achieve its goals. It is important to note that AI risk appetite is not a static concept. It can change over time as the enterprise's business, AI capabilities, and regulatory environment change.

By understanding the factors that influence an enterprise's AI risk appetite, companies can develop and implement appropriate AI risk management strategies.

WHAT ARE AI RISK-CONTROL EXAMPLES?

Key benefits of having a defined AI risk appetite include:

- **Increased confidence in AI risk-based, decision-making:** AI risk appetite helps companies to have confidence in the risk-based decisions made by AI systems. This is because the enterprise will understand the risks with AI and how they are managed.

- **Improved AI risk management:** AI risk appetite helps companies to improve their AI risk management practices. This is because the enterprise will understand the risks with AI and how they are mitigated.

- **Reduced costs:** AI risk appetite helps companies to reduce their costs. This is because the enterprise will be able to avoid costly mistakes and disruptions that can occur when AI systems are not properly managed.

WHY IT MATTERS?

By defining their AI risk appetite, companies reap benefits of AI while minimizing the AI risks.

AI RISK TOLERANCE

AI risk tolerance is the amount of risk that an AI system, project, or human is willing to accept when using AI. It is a measure of how much AI risk an individual is willing to take on to achieve his or her goals.

WHAT IS THE RISK?

It is important to note that AI risk tolerance is not a static concept. It can change over time as AI capabilities and regulatory environment change.

By understanding the factors that influence AI risk tolerance, humans can develop and deploy AI systems are both safe and effective.

WHAT ARE AI RISK-CONTROL EXAMPLES?

Factors that influence AI risk tolerance include:

- **Nature of the individual's business:** Humans like financial institutions are cautious about AI risks. They have a responsibility to protect their customers' money and assets, making them risk-averse.

- **Maturity of individual's AI capabilities:** Humans who are new to AI are cautious about taking AI risks. They lack experience and expertise in managing AI-related risks.

- **Regulatory environment:** The level of regulation in an industry can impact AI risk tolerance. Humans operating in heavily regulated industries, like healthcare, are risk-averse.

AI risk tolerance is not fixed and can change over time as the individual's situation evolves, including their AI capabilities and the regulatory environment they operate in.

WHY IT MATTERS?

By developing an AI risk tolerance that fits their unique situation, humans can use AI safely and effectively while minimizing the risk of loss. Humans can develop an AI risk tolerance that is appropriate for their situations. This will help them to use AI safely and effectively while minimizing the AI risk of loss. Benefits of defining AI risk tolerance for humans include:

- **Increased confidence in AI risk-based, decision-making:** Having a clear AI risk tolerance helps humans trust the risk-based decisions made by AI systems confidently.

- **Improved AI risk management:** AI risk tolerance allows humans to enhance their AI risk management practices.

- **Reduced costs:** By having a clear AI risk tolerance, humans can avoid costly mistakes and disruptions that occurs when AI systems are not properly managed.

AI RISK ATTITUDE

AI risk attitude is about how a human sees and deals with the potential dangers related to AI. It is a complex idea influenced by various things like human personality, the norms the human lives in, and past experiences with technology.

WHAT IS THE RISK?

As AI continues to advance and become widespread, our attitudes towards AI risks are likely to change. Understanding and considering these attitudes are crucial when humans create and use AI systems as it ensures that AI is used safely and responsibly.

There are two main types of AI risk attitudes:

- **Risk-averse:** Humans with a risk-averse attitude towards AI are worried about the potential risks of AI such as job loss, discrimination, and misuse of data. They are cautious about AI's development and use. They might support policies to regulate or limit AI.

- **Risk-taking:** Humans with a risk-taking attitude believe that the benefits of AI outweigh the risks. They support the development and use of AI and think it can help solve important global problems.

WHAT ARE AI RISK-CONTROL EXAMPLES?

It is essential to understand these attitudes and consider them while developing risk-controls and using AI. It ensures that AI is used responsibly and with proper safety measures. Several factors can influence AI risk attitude:

- **Individual personality traits:** Humans are naturally inclined to be cautious about AI risks. Personality can shape how a human perceives and handles AI-related risks.

- **Cultural norms:** Different cultures have different views on AI risks. Cultures might be accepting of these risks.

- **Experiences with technology:** If a human had bad experiences with technology or automated risk-based, decision-making in the past, the human might be likely to have a negative attitude towards AI risks. Conversely, positive experiences with technology make humans optimistic about AI's potential.

WHY IT MATTERS?

AI risk attitude is not a fixed or unchanging concept. As humans learn about AI and it becomes sophisticated, our attitudes towards AI risks can change over time. Different humans have varying attitudes towards AI risks depending on the specific applications of AI.

By understanding the factors that influence AI risk attitude, developers can create AI systems that are likely to be accepted and used by humans. This can help policymakers and regulators to address the concerns of those who are cautious or averse to AI risks. It is about making AI safer and accountable for everyone.

AI RISK PERCEPTION FACTORS

AI risk perception is how humans view and understand the potential risks with AI.

WHAT IS THE RISK?

AI residual risks include those that are still present even after a company has taken steps to reduce or control the potential dangers with AI. These risks can remain for various reasons. Ways of reducing AI risks may not be possible or practical. A company might not be able to completely avoid using AI and cannot transfer the risk of AI-related losses to someone else.

AI is a fast-evolving technology and the risks with AI are constantly changing. This can make it challenging for companies to keep up with the latest risks and implement effective measures to address them.

AI systems are also complex and not easily understandable. This makes it difficult for companies to understand how they work and identify potential risks making it hard to implement effective risk reduction measures.

Understanding AI risk perception is important because it impacts how humans respond to AI. If a human sees AI as risky, they might be less inclined to adopt AI technologies or use them responsibly.

WHAT ARE AI RISK-CONTROL EXAMPLES?

AI risk perception is about how humans see and understand the potential risks and controls with AI. It is influenced by several things such as:

- **Risk management framework:** An organization's risk management framework is a set of guidelines that helps them evaluate and handle risks including those related to AI. The organization's risk appetite or its willingness to take on certain risks shapes its risk management strategies, risk-controls, and measures to align with the level of risk it is comfortable with.

- **Individual characteristics:** Human individual traits like age, gender, education level, and personality can influence how a human perceives AI risks. Older humans worry about AI leading to job loss, while younger ones are excited about the potential for AI to create new job opportunities.

- **Media coverage**: How AI is portrayed in the media can impact how humans see AI risks. If the media talks about AI as a threat, humans are likely to perceive it as risky.

- **Personal experiences**: Personal encounters with AI can shape how humans perceive its risks. If a human had a bad experience with an AI system, he or she views AI as risky.

- **Cultural factors**: Cultural backgrounds can influence how humans perceive AI risks. In individualistic cultures AI might be seen as a threat, whereas in Asian cultures it might be seen as an opportunity.

- **Risk tolerance**: This is how willing an organization is to accept the negative impacts of AI risks. Organizations are daring and take on bigger risks for the chance of bigger rewards, while some are cautious and prefer safer approaches.

- **Risk appetite statements**: These are statements that define an organization's position on taking risks with AI. They set the limits within which the organization feels comfortable operating and the level of risk it is accepting.

- **Regulatory and legal considerations**: Organizations take into account the rules and laws related to AI. They follow these regulations to ensure that AI systems meet legal requirements and do not pose unnecessary risks or harm.

- **Ethical considerations**: These involve aligning AI systems with ethical principles like fairness, transparency, accountability, and respecting privacy and human rights. They show an organization's commitment to avoiding or minimizing AI risks that could lead to unethical or harmful outcomes.

- **Organizational objectives and outcomes**: Different organizations have different risk appetites based on their goals, market position, and the trade-offs between risk and reward. They consider the potential benefits of using AI for things like innovation, gaining a competitive edge, and creating value.

WHY IT MATTERS?

It is crucial to assure that AI is developed and used in ways that benefit humans. Companies can work on reducing the likelihood and consequence of AI risks by considering these perceptions and taking accountable actions to address them.

ENTERPRISE RISK APPETITE

An enterprise's AI risk attitude is how it deals with the potential risks related to AI. It is influenced by various factors like the company's size, industry, and culture.

WHAT IS THE RISK?

An enterprise's AI risk attitude can change over time as it learns about AI. Companies regularly review their AI risk attitude to make sure it is appropriate for their current situation.

Several factors influence an enterprise's AI risk appetite:

- **Size:** Larger companies tend to be cautious about AI risks because they have to lose if something goes wrong.

- **Industry:** Certain industries, like finance and healthcare, are risk-averse because they protect customer data and follow regulations.

- **Culture:** Cultures are cautious about AI risks. Japanese culture tends to be more risk-averse than American culture.

- **Nature of the business:** Businesses dealing with finances or customer assets are cautious about AI risks because they protect their clients' money and belongings.

- **Maturity of AI capabilities:** Newcomers to AI are cautious because they lack experience in managing AI risks.

- **Regulatory environment:** The level of regulation in an industry can influence how cautious a company is about AI risks. Heavily regulated industries are risk-averse.

WHAT ARE AI RISK-CONTROL EXAMPLES?

To develop a positive or risk-taking AI risk attitude, companies can take several steps:

- **Educate employees about AI:** Companies provide knowledge and information about AI to their employees. When employees understand AI, they are likely to support its use.

- **Create a culture of innovation:** Encouraging employees to be innovative and try out new technologies including AI results in a positive attitude towards AI adoption.

- **Set clear goals and expectations:** Companies communicate clearly with their employees about how AI is used and what is expected of them when using it.

- **Provide training and support:** Proper training on how to use AI safely and responsibly is crucial. Employees can then have the skills and knowledge to work with AI effectively.

- **Monitor and review:** Companies regularly assess and review their AI risk management strategies to ensure they remain effective.

WHY IT MATTERS?

By understanding these influencing factors, companies can develop and implement appropriate strategies to manage AI risks effectively.

When companies develop and implement an AI risk management framework aligned with their AI risk appetite, they can achieve their goals while minimizing the risk of potential losses. This approach helps them make the most of AI's benefits while responsibly managing its risks.

AI RISK RESILIENCE

AI risk resilience is the ability of an enterprise to withstand the consequence of AI risks. It is important for companies to be resilient to AI risks because AI is a rapidly evolving technology and the risks with AI are constantly changing.

AI Risk Appetite

WHAT IS THE RISK?

AI risk resilience is the ability of a company to handle and withstand the impact of AI risks. AI risk resilience involves:

- **Reduced AI risk:** By being resilient to AI risks, companies can reduce their exposure to AI risk. This protects companies from financial losses, reputational damage, and other negative impacts.

- **Improved decision-making:** By understanding the risks with AI, companies can make risk-based decisions about how to use AI. This helps companies to improve their efficiency, accuracy, and decision-making.

- **Increased trust:** By being resilient to AI risks, companies can build trust with their customers, employees, and other stakeholders. This helps companies to attract and retain customers, employees, and investors.

WHAT ARE AI RISK-CONTROL EXAMPLES?

Additional tips for companies to increase their AI risk resilience through risk-controls are:

- **Build a culture of AI risk awareness:** Companies create a culture where employees are aware of AI risks and feel comfortable reporting potential risks they identify.

- **Invest in AI risk management tools:** Using AI risk management tools help companies identify and mitigate potential AI risks effectively.

- **Partner with experts:** Companies benefit from partnering with specialized AI risk management firms that offer guidance and support in developing and implementing effective AI risk management strategies.

Why It Matters?

AI risk resilience offers several benefits:

- **Reduced AI risk:** By being resilient to AI risks, companies can lower their exposure to potential negative impacts such as financial losses and damage to their reputation.

- **Improved risk-based, decision-making:** Understanding AI risks allows companies to make risk-based decisions about how to use AI leading to improved efficiency, accuracy, and overall decision-making.

- **Increased trust:** Resilience to AI risks helps companies build trust with customers, employees, and stakeholders. This can attract and retain customers, employees, and investors.

WHY IT MATTERS?

Increasing AI risk resilience allows companies to design protections from potential negative impacts related to AI, ensuring they can navigate the ever-changing landscape of AI technology.

AI RISK BENEFIT

It is important to weigh the benefits and costs of taking on an AI risk before making a risk-based decision.

WHAT IS THE RISK?

By doing an AI risk-benefit analysis, a human can make risk-based decisions about whether to take on AI risks. After a human has assessed and addressed AI risks, he or she can determine if the remaining risks are acceptable. This process is called an AI risk-benefit analysis. To do this, the human considers the advantages of taking on the AI risk and the potential drawbacks.

The benefits of taking on AI risks include:

- Chance of making a profit.

- Chance of achieving a goal.

- Chance of learning something new.

The costs of taking on an AI risk can involve:

- Chance of losing money.
- Possibility of not achieving the desired goal.
- Risk of getting hurt or experiencing negative outcomes.

WHAT ARE AI RISK-CONTROL EXAMPLES?

Factors to consider during an AI risk-benefit analysis are:

- **Personal values:** What matters most to the human and aligns with their principles.
- **Financial situation:** How much money they can afford to invest or potentially lose.
- **AI risk tolerance:** How comfortable they are with taking on risks related to AI.
- **Laws and regulations:** Ensuring that the risk-based decision complies with relevant rules and regulations.

WHY IT MATTERS?

By thoughtfully conducting an AI risk-benefit analysis, humans can make informed decisions about whether it is worthwhile to take on AI risks

KEY POINTS

- Risk appetite is an organizations or human's willingness or ability to accept a level of AI risk.
- AI risk attitude is how a human sees and deals with AI dangers.
- AI perception is similar to risk attitude but relates to how a human or company sees AI as either beneficial or dangerous.
- Humans see AI as a benefit such as a chance of making a profit or reaching a goal.

- Residual risk is the risk left over after a company has taken steps to reduce known risks.

- Enterprise risk is the organization's risk attitude regarding risk-controls and residual risk.

- Enterprise risk appetite is the amount of AI risk the organization is willing to take.

- AI risk tolerance is the amount of AI risk a human is willing to accept.

- AI risk resilience is the ability of a company to withstand the impact of AI risks.

AI RISK TREATMENT

WHAT IS THE KEY IDEA IN THIS CHAPTER?

AI risk treatment is the process of implementing measures, risk-controls, and actions to manage, mitigate, or control risks with AI systems. Risk treatment measures will depend on the nature of the AI system, identified risks, organization's risk appetite, regulatory requirements, and ethical considerations. The best approach to AI risk treatment will vary depending on the AI risks that an enterprise faces.

AI RISK MANAGEMENT PROCESSES

The AI risk management process can be thought of a risk management framework consisting of a systematic approach to identifying, assessing, and mitigating the risks with AI risk controls.

WHAT IS THE RISK?

Risk-controls are things that companies do to mitigate AI risks. AI risk sources are things that can cause harm or loss to an enterprise. Events are things that happen that can lead to AI risks. Outcomes are the things that could happen if an AI risk materializes.

AI risk-control is the process of implementing measures to reduce the likelihood or consequence of AI risks with AI. It is an important part of any enterprise's AI risk management process. The best approach to AI risk-control will vary depending on the AI risks that an enterprise faces.

WHAT ARE AI RISK-CONTROL EXAMPLES?

Here are examples of how companies can mitigate the AI risks using human behavior and culture as risk-controls:

- **Use ethical AI principles:** There are ethical AI principles that companies can follow. These principles can help companies to design AI systems that are fair, safe, and responsible.

- **Ensure AI systems are transparent and accountable:** Transparency and accountability build trust between AI developers and humans.

- **Build in guardrails and safeguards:** Companies can build in safeguards to their AI systems to prevent them from being used in harmful ways. They can use machine learning to identify and prevent fake news.

- **Start with a clear understanding of the enterprise's use of AI:** Identify what AI systems are currently in use and what AI systems are planned for the future.

- **Use high-quality data:** The data is free of most bias and representative of the population that the AI system will be used on.

- **Identify the potential risks with AI:** Look at what are the potential harms that AI can cause and what are the potential sources of these harms.

- **Assess the likelihood and consequence of each AI risk:** Assess how likely each AI risk occurs and what would be the consequence of each AI risk if it did occur.

- **Develop a plan to mitigate the AI risks:** Look at what measures are taken to reduce the likelihood or consequence of each AI risk.

- **Implement the plan and monitor its effectiveness:** Review if the plan is working and if any changes have to be made.

- **Educate humans:** Companies can educate humans about the potential AI risks of AI systems.

WHY IT MATTERS?

By following these best practices, companies can improve their ability to manage AI risk and protect their assets, operations, and reputation.

AI RMF PROCESSES

Companies have a process for identifying, assessing, and managing AI risks. This process is a risk management framework. This process is AI risk-based specifically meaning that it focuses on the AI risks that are most likely to occur and that would have the biggest impacts on the enterprise.

WHAT IS THE RISK?

Risk management involves identifying, analyzing, evaluating, and responding to risks. This can include avoiding risk, reducing or mitigating risk, transferring risk through insurance or contracts, and accepting or tolerating risk.

Positive risks known as opportunities can bring favorable outcomes or benefits. These can arise from innovation, technology advancements, market trends, or strategic decisions. Understanding and managing risks are essential for making informed decisions, achieving goals, and dealing with uncertainties.

WHAT ARE AI RISK-CONTROL EXAMPLES?

There are various risk-control strategies to treating AI risks:

- **AI risk avoidance:** Companies choose not to use AI if they are worried about the risks or lack the resources to manage them effectively.

- **AI risk reduction:** Companies decrease the likelihood or consequence of AI risks by training AI systems on diverse data using security measures against hacking and ensuring safety and security monitoring.

- **AI risk transfer:** Transferring AI risks to another party is through insurance or employing a third-party to manage AI systems.

WHY IT MATTERS?

Treating AI risks is crucial for companies to effectively manage the risks with AI. The benefits of treating AI risks include:

- **Reduced AI risk:** Taking appropriate steps to treat AI risks lowers the chances of those risks occurring or reduces their consequence. This protects companies from financial losses, damage to their reputations, and other negative impacts.

- **Improved risk-based, decision-making:** Understanding AI risks allows companies to make risk-based decisions about using AI leading to increased efficiency and accuracy.

- **Increased trust:** Treating AI risks builds trust with their customers, employees, and stakeholders. This fosters loyalty and helps attract and retain customers, employees, and investors.

There are challenges in AI risk treatment such as the complexity of AI risks, the constantly changing nature of AI risks, and the potential high costs involved. These challenges make it difficult for companies especially smaller ones to identify, assess, and address AI risks effectively.

Despite the challenges, AI risk treatment remains a crucial aspect of any enterprise's AI risk management process. It creates a safer and accountable AI environment for everyone involved.

RISK TREATMENT PLANS

Once an AI risk treatment plan is made, a human needs to implement it. This means taking the steps that are outlined in the risk treatment plan. It is important to monitor the implementation of the AI risk treatment plan to make sure that it works appropriately.

To develop an AI risk treatment plan, a human needs to identify the AI risks and then create a comprehensive strategy to effectively implement the chosen treatment option. This process is called AI risk treatment planning.

WHAT IS THE RISK?

Once a plan to treat AI risks is created, it is crucial to put it into action by following the steps outlined in the plan. Monitoring the implementation of the plan is important to ensure that everything is progressing as intended.

An AI risk treatment plan includes various components such as a description of the context surrounding AI, a clear explanation of the specific AI risk, the chosen treatment option, the steps required for implementation, necessary resources, a timeline for execution, and a way to measure the success of the AI risk treatment option.

After the AI risk treatment plan is implemented, its effectiveness is evaluated. This means measuring whether the AI risk treatment option has been successful in reducing the likelihood or consequence of the AI risk. Once a human has identified AI risk, a plan in place is developed to make sure that the chosen AI risk treatment option is implemented effectively.

WHAT ARE AI RISK-CONTROL EXAMPLES?

An AI risk treatment plan includes the following:

- Description of the context surrounding AI.
- Description of the AI risk.
- Chosen AI risk treatment option.
- Steps taken to implement the AI risk treatment option.
- Resources needed to implement the AI risk treatment option.
- Timeline for implementing the AI risk treatment option.
- Success of the AI risk treatment option will be measured.

WHY IT MATTERS?

If the AI risk treatment option has not been successful, the plan is revised and a new AI risk treatment option is implemented.

Evaluating the effectiveness of the AI risk treatment option is crucial. If the treatment option proves to be unsuccessful, it might be necessary to revise the plan or consider a different AI risk treatment approach. Regular assessment and adjustments are essential to maintain a safe and accountable AI environment.

AI RISK AVOIDANCE

AI risk aversion is the tendency to avoid or be hesitant to adopt AI technologies due to concerns about the potential risks with these technologies.

WHAT IS THE RISK?

AI risk aversion is the tendency of humans to be hesitant or avoid using AI technologies because of concerns about potential risks with these technologies.

AI risk aversion can pose an obstacle to the widespread adoption of AI technologies. To address these concerns, it is essential to develop AI systems that are transparent, accountable, and safe. Educating humans about both the potential risks and benefits of AI empowers them to make informed decisions regarding the adoption of these technologies.

WHAT ARE AI RISK-CONTROL EXAMPLES?

Risk aversion is a form of risk-control. Humans are by nature risk-averse towards AI due to several reasons:

- **Lack of understanding:** Humans do not understand how AI functions or the potential risks it entails leading to fear of the unknown and reluctance to embrace AI.

- **Concerns about fairness:** Humans worry that AI could be used in a manner that is unfair or discriminatory. AI systems might influence risk-based decisions about hiring, lending, or insurance, disproportionately impacting certain groups.

- **Fear of job loss:** Humans are concerned that AI advancements will lead to job displacement. While automation might replace jobs, it is crucial to focus on upskilling and reskilling to prepare for the new opportunities AI creates.

- **Security concerns:** There are worries about the security of AI systems. Given the complexity of AI, there is a potential vulnerability to hacking, leading to data theft or manipulation of AI systems.

WHY IT MATTERS?

The level of AI risk is influenced by the specific application of AI. AI systems used to control autonomous vehicles or critical systems have a higher risk of harm compared to AI systems used for generating marketing content.

AI RISK RETENTION

AI risk retention is a risk management strategy in which an enterprise chooses to bear the risk of AI losses itself. Risk retention is the same as risk acceptance in many cases. This is done through a variety of mechanisms such as self-insurance, captive insurance, and AI risk pooling.

WHAT IS THE RISK?

AI risk retention is a strategy in risk management where a company chooses to bear the potential losses from AI risks itself. They do this through different methods such as self-insurance, captive insurance, or pooling AI risks.

Companies opt for AI risk retention because they believe the cost of transferring or mitigating AI risk is too high. They feel confident in their ability to handle AI risks effectively.

AI risk retention can offer several advantages for companies including saving costs, having control over risk management, and being able to customize their risk management approach according to their specific needs.

There are challenges with AI risk retention including the potential for financial losses, damage to the company's reputation, and legal liability if AI risks result in losses. There are reasons why companies might choose to retain AI risk. Companies believe that the cost of transferring or mitigating AI risk is too high.

WHAT ARE AI RISK-CONTROL EXAMPLES?

Risk reduction is a form of risk-control. Here are ways for reducing AI risk exposure:

- **Design AI systems to be robust and reliable:** AI systems are designed to be resistant to failure and misuse.

- **Develop AI systems that are transparent and accountable:** AI systems are designed that allow humans to understand how they work and why they make the risk-based decisions they do. They are designed so it allows them to be audited and held accountable for their actions.

- **Educate the public about AI:** The public is educated about the potential benefits and risks of AI. This includes explaining how AI systems work, how they are used, and how they can be misused.

- **Develop international standards for the development and use of AI:** This would assure that AI systems are developed and used so that they are safe, responsible, and beneficial to humans.

WHY IT MATTERS?

AI risk retention can provide benefits for companies including:

- **Cost savings:** Companies can avoid the cost of transferring or mitigating AI risk.

- **Control:** Companies have control over how that AI risk is managed.

- **Flexibility:** Companies can tailor their AI risk management strategy to their needs.

Despite these challenges, AI risk retention is an effective way to manage the AI risks of AI. By considering the AI risks and benefits, companies can make an informed decision about retaining AI risk. Despite the challenges, AI risk retention is a viable way to manage AI risks. Companies assess the potential risks and benefits to make informed decisions about retaining AI risk.

AI RISK ACCEPTANCE

WHAT IS THE RISK?

Risk acceptance is a form of risk-control. AI risk acceptance is the risk-based decision to accept AI risks. This is done for reasons including:

- **Benefits of AI outweigh the AI risks:** The benefits of using AI are so great that companies are willing to accept the risks. AI is used to improve efficiency, accuracy, and decision-making.

- **Risks of AI are low:** The risks of AI are low enough that companies are willing to accept them. The risk of an AI system making a mistake is low if the system is carefully designed and thoroughly tested.

- **Costs of mitigating the AI risks are too high:** The costs of mitigating the risks of AI are too high. It is too expensive to develop and implement security measures to protect AI systems from hacking.

WHY IT MATTERS?

By understanding the AI risks, companies can make informed decisions about accepting those AI risks. AI risk acceptance is the choice of a company to embrace the potential risks with AI technology.

AI RISK-CONTROLS

Risk-controls are actions or measures that companies implement to reduce the potential risks with AI. AI risk sources are factors or elements that have the potential to cause harm or loss to a company. Events are incidents or occurrences that can lead to AI risks. Outcomes are the results or consequences that arise if an AI risk becomes a reality.

WHAT IS THE RISK?

AI risk-control is the process of taking steps to lower the likelihood or consequence of AI risks related to AI technology. It plays a critical role in managing and mitigating risks for any company using AI. Risk-controls are used to mitigate AI risks by reducing the likelihood of an AI risk occurring and minimizing the consequence of an AI risk if it does occur.

The most suitable approach to AI risk-control will differ based on the specific AI risks faced by a company. Nevertheless, companies have a plan in place to control AI risks.

To control AI risks, a company identifies relevant risk-controls that are applied during the development or use of AI. These risk-controls are found in internal systems, procedures, audit reports, or discovered during the AI risk management process.

Risk-controls are used to mitigate AI risks by either reducing the chances of an AI risk occurring or minimizing the negative consequences if the risk does manifest.

WHAT ARE AI RISK-CONTROL EXAMPLES?

AI risk-controls are measures that companies implement to reduce AI risks and protect from potential harm. The company assesses the effectiveness of these identified risk-controls to ensure that they are functioning as intended and being followed by employees. Examples of AI risk-controls include:

- **Policies:** These are sets of rules and procedures established by the company to guide its actions and risk-based decisions related to AI.

- **Procedures:** These are step-by-step instructions that outline how specific tasks related to AI management are carried out.

- **Training:** By providing employees with the necessary knowledge and skills they can perform their jobs safely and effectively.

- **Supervision:** Monitoring employees ensures they are following company policies and procedures related to AI

- **Audits:** Regular reviews of the company's systems and risk-controls ensure they are effective and comply with AI risk management standards.

- **Incident response plans:** Detailed plans that outline how the company can respond in the event of AI-related incidents or risks.

WHY IT MATTERS?

Despite the challenges, implementing AI risk-controls is crucial for companies to reduce the likelihood and consequence of AI risks. By identifying and addressing potential risks, companies can mitigate harmful AI risks while maximizing the benefits of AI technology.

Controlling AI risks is essential for companies to effectively manage the potential negative impacts of AI.

Benefits of AI Risk-Control:

- **Reduced AI risk:** Implementing AI risk-controls helps companies decrease the likelihood or consequence of AI-related risks. This shields them from financial losses, damage to reputation, and other adverse impacts.

- **Improved risk-based, decision-making:** Understanding AI risks allows companies to make informed choices about how to use AI. This leads to enhanced efficiency, accuracy, and overall risk-based decision-making.

- **Increased trust:** By proactively controlling AI risks, companies build trust with customers, employees, and stakeholders. This fosters loyalty and attracts business and investment opportunities.

Challenges in AI Risk-Control:

- **Complexity:** AI risks are intricate and challenging to understand making it difficult for companies to identify and assess them properly.

- **Constant Change:** The risks with AI are evolving, which means companies continuously update their AI risk-control strategies to stay effective.

- **Cost:** Implementing AI risk-controls are costly creating financial obstacles for smaller companies.

RISK SHARING

AI risk sharing is an approach to AI risk management that involves sharing the risk of AI losses among multiple stakeholders. This is done through a variety of mechanisms such as insurance, annuities, or mutual funds.

WHAT IS THE RISK?

There are reasons why companies might choose to share AI risks. AI systems are becoming increasingly complex and sophisticated making it difficult for any enterprise to understand and manage the AI risks with them. The potential for AI losses is increasing as AI systems are used in critical applications.

Reasons for AI risk sharing include:

- **Complexity of AI systems:** AI technology is becoming advanced making it challenging for handling all the AI risks.

- **Increasing AI losses:** As AI is used in critical applications, the possibility of AI-related losses rises.

WHAT ARE AI RISK-CONTROL EXAMPLES?

Risk sharing is a form of risk-control. Examples of AI risk sharing include:

- **Identifying partners:** After developing an AI risk management plan, potential partners are identified who are willing to share the AI risk.

- **Negotiating an agreement:** A risk-sharing agreement is created with the terms, such as how much risk each party will share and the process for resolving disputes.

- **Monitoring the agreement:** Regularly reviewing the risk-sharing agreement ensures it remains effective and correctly implemented.

Challenges of AI Risk Sharing:

- **Complexity:** AI risks are intricate making it hard for companies to identify and assess them properly.

- **Constant Change:** AI risks evolve over time requiring companies to update their risk-sharing arrangements.

- **Cost:** AI risk sharing is costly especially for smaller companies.

WHY IT MATTERS?

Despite these challenges, AI risk sharing is an effective way to manage AI risks. Overcoming these obstacles allows companies to enhance their ability to protect potential AI-related harm and maximize the benefits of AI technology.

AI RISK RESOURCES

Companies can take steps to mitigate AI risks by staying current and talking with stakeholders about AI outcomes and risks.

WHAT IS THE RISK?

Potential outcomes refer to the possible results or impacts that could occur if an AI risk becomes a reality. These outcomes are either tangible, which means they are measured or quantified like financial losses or property damage. Or, they can be intangible, which means they cannot be easily measured like reputational damage or loss of trust.

WHAT ARE AI RISK-CONTROL EXAMPLES?

To identify potential outcomes, various risk-control sources can be used:

- **Published standards:** Organizations like ISO, ANSI, NIST, and IEEE have established AI systems standards.

- **Technical specifications:** Similar to published standards, organizations like ISO, ANSI, NIST, and IEEE have developed technical standards, specifications, and guidelines for AI systems.

- **Scientific papers:** Research articles that present findings from studies on AI systems provide valuable insights.

- **Market data:** Data highlighting how AI systems are used in the market offer a glimpse of potential outcomes.

- **Reports of incidents:** Learning from past incidents involving AI systems shed light on potential risks.

- **Field trials:** Testing AI systems in real-world scenarios provide valuable data on their performance.

- **Usability studies:** Conducting studies to evaluate how easily humans use AI systems.

- **Results of appropriate investigations:** Findings from investigations into AI risks can help identify potential outcomes.

- **Stakeholder reports:** Reports submitted by customers, employees, and suppliers can provide valuable feedback.

- **Interviews and reports from experts:** Input from experts like engineers, scientists, and lawyers offer valuable insights.

- **Simulations:** Using computer models to simulate how AI systems might behave in different situations help predict potential outcomes.

WHY IT MATTERS?

By considering these methods and sources, companies understand and prepare for the potential outcomes with AI risks.

KEY POINTS

- Risk treatment is the same as risk management and risk mitigation.

- Risk treatment is the process of implementing risk-controls to manage, mitigate, and risk-controls to manage risks.

- Companies need a process often a risk management framework to manage risks.

- Risk treatment plans are a part of the risk management framework.

- Risk avoidance is the process to avoid AI systems due to their inherent risks.

- Risk retention is the risk management strategy to accept AI risks.

- Risk mitigation is the application of risk-control to manage risks.

- Risk management is used in place of risk treatment. The application of risk management framework is called risk management.

- AI risk-controls are action to reduce AI risks.

- AI risk sharing is the strategy to share risks with multiple humans and stakeholders.

AI CONFORMITY ASSESSMENT

WHAT IS THE KEY IDEA IN THIS CHAPTER?

AI conformity assessment is a process of evaluating and monitoring whether an AI system complies with relevant laws, regulations, and technical standards. AI conformity assessment is the basis for AI risk-assurance and accountability. Conformity assessment is the basis for trusting AI software and systems. It is an important part of any enterprise's AI risk management program.

AI conformity assessment is evolving. It may involve self-declaration, product watermarks, trust labels, or third-party audits. Another book in the Trust series will be written on AI conformity assessment since the EU is still developing guidelines.

AI VULNERABILITIES AND RISK ASSURANCE

AI vulnerability is how easily an AI system can be harmed, attacked, or taken advantage of. Moreover, AI systems are used for risk-based decisions with ethical implications, such as loan approvals or job hiring with high consequences in humans' lives. This requires careful consideration of the ethical aspects of AI risk assurance.

WHAT IS THE RISK?

AI vulnerability is a serious concern and it is crucial to take measures to reduce these risks. Ways to mitigate AI vulnerability include secure data collection and storage practices to prevent data poisoning, implementing secure training practices to avoid model stealing, physically securing AI systems to prevent physical attacks, and considering ethical implications when using AI for risk-based, decision-making.

By taking these precautions, humans can protect AI systems from potential harm and ensure they are used responsibly and ethically. By taking steps to mitigate AI vulnerability, AI systems are assured they are used safely and responsibly.

There are several types of threats that can make AI systems vulnerable and require assurance:

- **Model inversion:** Attackers try to reverse engineer the AI model to understand how it works or generate data to trick the model.

- **Data poisoning:** Attackers intentionally corrupt the data used to train the AI system leading to incorrect or biased predictions.

- **Evasion:** Attackers provide the AI system with crafted data to make it produce errors.

- **Model stealing:** Attackers steal the AI model to use it for their purposes or create their own AI system.

- **Physical attack:** Attackers physically damage or destroy the AI system rendering it useless or causing harm.

- **Physical tampering:** AI systems are physically tampered with, which can disrupt their operation or even cause them to malfunction.

- **Software vulnerabilities:** AI systems are software, and like all software they are susceptible to software vulnerabilities. Attackers exploit these vulnerabilities to gain control of the system or to disrupt its operation.

WHAT ARE AI RISK-CONTROL EXAMPLES?

AI vulnerabilities are a serious concern, but there are risk-control steps that can be taken to mitigate them. These steps include:

- **Using secure data collection and storage practices:** This can prevent data bias and model hacking.

- **Using secure training practices:** This can prevent model hacking and physical tampering.

- **Physically securing AI systems:** This can prevent physical tampering.

- **Keeping AI systems up to date with the latest security patches:** This can protect against software vulnerabilities.

- **Monitor AI systems for signs of malicious activity:** This includes monitoring for unusual patterns of behavior such as an AI system making a large number of incorrect or suspicious decisions.

WHY IT MATTERS?

Addressing AI vulnerabilities is crucial because it assures that AI systems are trusted and can be relied upon.

CONFORMITY ASSESSMENT OBJECTIVES

AI vulnerabilities can be exploited. This means that AI systems must be risk-assured. By considering these, companies can identify potential risks with AI systems and take steps to mitigate those AI risks and assure these systems are used in a safe and accountable way.

WHAT IS THE RISK?

When identifying risks with AI systems, it is important to consider the objectives of the AI system and the context in which it is used.

WHAT ARE AI RISK-CONTROL EXAMPLES?

AI risk-controls should consider:

- **Purpose of the AI system:** Understanding its intended function is crucial for assessing potential risks.

- **Intended users of the AI system:** Knowing the users and their needs helps in evaluating the risks specific to them and the data used for training and operating the AI system. Ensuring that the data is accurate and complete is vital to prevent biased or incorrect outcomes.

- **Environment of AI system usage:** The surroundings or conditions can influence the AI system. Factors like different environments or human behaviors can impact the AI system's performance.

- **Potential impacts of the AI system:** Considering the possible impacts of failure is essential to prepare for potential risks.

WHY IT MATTERS?

The objective to AI conformity assessment can be accountability or trust. For example, when a human buys products, there may be an AI trust label such as a safety guarantee. When a human buys food, there is a contents label. When a human buys a lawnmower, there is a user manual and other trust material such as safety use warning. When a human buys an electrical product, there is an UL label or CE mark, which convey trust. For many products and services, there is implicit trust such as when a human turns on the stove, that the natural gas is safe and will work. When the human flies, he or she trusts the pilot and airline to get the human to the destination is assumed.

By considering these factors, companies can effectively identify and manage AI risks, ensuring that their AI systems operate safely and ethically.

AI ACCOUNTABILTY

Accountability is about being responsible for actions such as architecting, designing, and deploying the AI system. It means that a human can explain why something was done and that the human is willing to face the consequences of his or her actions.

WHAT IS THE RISK?

Accountability is about taking responsibility for the actions and risk-based decisions made when creating and using AI systems. It means being able to explain why certain choices were made and being willing to face the consequences of those choices.

In the context of AI systems, accountability requires companies being responsible for the actions and risk-based decisions of their AI systems. They can explain why their AI systems made specific decisions and be ready to accept the consequences if their systems cause harm.

AI accountability involves understanding and explaining how AI systems make risk-based decisions. This includes identifying the factors that influenced a decision and understanding the potential outcomes of that risk-based decision. It is crucial for ensuring that AI systems are used in a responsible and ethical manner.

Key aspects of AI accountability include:

- **Transparency:** AI systems are transparent in how they make risk-based decisions. Humans can understand the reasoning behind AI-driven choices.

- **Explainability:** AI systems and developers can explain risk-based decisions so humans can understand. Humans understand the factors contributing to a decision and its possible consequences.

- **Clear responsibility:** There are clear lines of responsibility for AI system decisions ensuring that humans are held accountable for the system's actions.

- **Fair usage:** By requiring companies to explain their AI systems' decisions, accountability ensures that the technology is not used in a discriminatory or harmful manner.

- **Safety:** Regular monitoring and auditing of AI systems help identify and address any potential issues to ensure their safe operation.

- **Compensation for harm:** A process for addressing complaints about AI systems ensures that those harmed by the technology are compensated for their losses.

WHAT ARE AI RISK-CONTROL EXAMPLES?

There is no one-size-fits-all solution for AI accountability as the approach varies depending on the nature and complexity of the AI system. Nevertheless, by considering these key aspects and implementing appropriate risk-control measures, companies can assure that their AI systems are used in a responsible and ethical manner

To assure AI accountability, companies can take specific measures to ensure that their AI systems are used responsibly and ethically. Here are ways to implement AI accountability:

- **Clear policies and procedures:** Companies establish clear policies and procedures for the development and use of AI systems. These policies include requirements for transparency, explainability, and fairness, ensuring that the risk-based, decision-making process is understandable and fair.

- **Monitoring and auditing:** Companies have a process for regularly monitoring and auditing their AI systems. This helps identify any potential issues or biases in the system and allows for corrective actions to be taken.

- **Logging:** AI system developers keep detailed logs of their risk-based decisions and actions. This helps track the decision-making process and allows for understanding and analysis of the system's behavior.

- **Explainable AI:** Techniques that make AI risk-based decisions explainable are employed. This helps humans understand how the AI arrived at a particular decision enhancing trust and accountability.

- **Risk-based auditing:** AI systems are subjected to risk-based auditing, which means assessing the potential risks with the system and conducting audits accordingly.

- **Fair complaint response process:** Companies have a fair and impartial process for handling complaints related to their AI systems. This ensures that any harm caused by the AI system is properly addressed and compensated.

WHY IT MATTERS?

AI accountability is crucial because it ensures that AI systems are developed and used so it benefits companies and humans. It builds trust in AI technologies and helps prevent potential negative consequences that could arise from irresponsible AI practices. By embracing AI accountability, companies can contribute to the responsible advancement and deployment of AI systems.

AI ASSURANCE

When companies use AI, they track how it is being used. This is because AI can impact the way they interact with the technology. If an AI system is used to make risk-based

AI Conformity Assessment

decisions about who gets a loan, it is important to track how are using the system to make sure that it is fair and accurate.

WHAT IS THE RISK?

Companies that develop AI systems keep track of any information that is available about how the system might be used in the future. Companies that use AI systems maintain records of how the systems are used throughout the lifetime of the system. This information can help companies to identify any potential problems with the system and to make sure that the system is used in a safe and responsible way.

WHAT ARE AI RISK-CONTROL EXAMPLES?

Examples of how companies can track AI use include:

- **Conduct user surveys:** These surveys can help companies to understand who are using AI systems and to identify any potential problems.

- **Monitor social media:** Social media is a good source of information about how the AI systems are used.

- **Track data usage:** Companies can track how AI uses data systems. This information can help companies to identify any potential problems with the system.

- **Establish clear policies and procedures:** Companies create clear rules and guidelines for developing and using AI systems. These policies include requirements for transparency, explainability, and fairness ensuring that the risk-based, decision-making process is understandable and fair.

- **Monitor and audit AI systems:** Regularly tracking of AI systems' performance and conducting audits can help identify potential issues or biases in the system. This allows companies to take corrective actions promptly.

- **Keep Detailed Logs:** AI systems maintain detailed records of their risk-based decisions and actions. This helps track the decision-making process and allows better understanding and analysis of the system's behavior.

- **Use explainable AI techniques:** Employ techniques that make AI risk-based decisions explainable. This ensures that humans can understand how the AI arrived at a particular decision, which enhances trust and accountability

- **Implement risk-based auditing:** Assess the potential risks with the AI system and conduct audits accordingly. This helps focus on areas with higher risks and potential consequences.

- **Have a fair complaint response process:** Establish a fair and impartial process for handling complaints related to the AI system. This ensures that any harm caused by the AI system is appropriately addressed and compensated.

There is no one-size-fits-all approach to AI accountability as each AI system has unique characteristics and risks. By considering these key aspects and implementing suitable measures, companies can ensure that their AI systems are used responsibly and ethically.

WHY IT MATTERS?

AI accountability is crucial because it guarantees that AI systems are developed and used in ways that benefit companies and humans. It fosters trust in AI technologies and prevents potential negative consequences that could arise from irresponsible AI practices. Embracing AI accountability allows companies to contribute to the responsible advancement and deployment of AI systems ensuring their safe and beneficial use.

MANAGING AI ASSURANCE AND ACCOUNTABILITY

In the EU, conformity assessment is the basis for AI accountability and AI assurance. AI conformity assessment is an important part of any enterprise's AI risk management strategy. It can assure that AI systems are used in an accountable and ethical way and that they do not pose any AI risks to humans.

WHAT IS THE RISK?

The EU AI Act emphasizes risk-based conformity assessment particularly for high-risk AI systems. This means that AI systems with higher potential for harm will face stringent risk assessments to guarantee their safety and adherence to regulations.

WHAT ARE AI RISK-CONTROL EXAMPLES?

Here are the steps that companies can take to implement AI conformity assessment:

- **Establish an AI conformity assessment team:** The first step is to form a team responsible for conducting AI conformity assessments.

- **Identify relevant AI laws, regulations, and technical standards:** Companies determine the laws, regulations, and technical standards that apply to their AI systems.

- **Assess the AI system's compliance with the identified rules:** The AI system is then evaluated against the applicable laws, regulations, and technical standards to check if it meets the required criteria.

- **Address any non-compliance issues:** If the AI system is found to have gaps in compliance and assurance, measures are taken to correct these issues. This might involve implementing new policies, providing additional training to employees, or making necessary changes to the AI system.

- **Develop conformity assessment methodology:** This is the specific approach or framework used to conduct the AI conformity assessment. It might involve using risk-based methodologies to focus on high-risk AI systems ensuring that they undergo thorough assessment and evaluation.

- **Conduct regular AI conformity assessments:** Companies perform these assessments regularly to ensure that their AI systems meet the required laws, regulations, and technical standards.

- **Conduct AI risk assessments:** These assessments identify potential risks with using AI systems.

- **Implement risk-controls:** To mitigate AI risks, companies put in place measures and risk-controls to manage potential issues.

- **Address non-compliance findings:** If any areas are found to be non-compliant, companies take action to fix them. This might involve updating policies, providing training to employees, or making changes to the AI system.

- **Monitor and review:** Companies continuously monitor and review their AI systems to make sure they are effectively managing AI risks.

WHY IT MATTERS?

AI conformity assessment is essential for holding AI systems accountable, protecting users and humans, and ensuring that AI technology is used responsibly and ethically. Implementing AI conformity assessment is crucial because it helps companies protect from the potential negative impacts of using AI. By following these steps, companies can ensure their AI systems are safe, compliant, and trustworthy.

AI RISK MONITORING

The risks with AI systems can change over time due to changes in the external and internal context of a company. If a company modifies its business model, new AI risks might arise for the AI system. AI owner and stakeholders can identify these dynamic AI risks and update the AI system to address them.

WHAT IS THE RISK?

AI monitoring is the continuous observation and assessment of AI systems' performance, behavior, processes, and outcomes. It helps organizations proactively identify and address potential issues, maintain system fairness and performance, uphold ethical standards, and build trust in AI technologies. AI risk monitoring focuses specifically on continuously assessing and managing the risks with AI making it a crucial part of any company's AI risk management program.

WHAT ARE RISK-CONTROL EXAMPLES

AI risk monitoring is an essential risk-control process and includes several steps:

- **Identifying AI risks:** The first step is to identify the potential risks with the AI system, which can be done through an AI risk assessment.

- **Evaluating AI risks:** Once identified, the AI risks are evaluated including assessing their likelihood and consequences.

- **Establish an AI risk management team:** Establish an AI risk management team. This team is responsible for identifying, evaluating, monitoring, and reporting AI risks.

- **Develop an AI risk management plan:** The AI risk management team develops an AI risk management plan. This plan outlines the steps that the enterprise will take to identify, evaluate, monitor, and report AI risks.

- **Implement AI risk mitigation measures:** The AI risk management plan includes a list of AI risk mitigation measures. These measures are designed to reduce the likelihood and consequence of AI risks.

- **Train employees:** Employees are trained on the risks with AI and how to identify and report potential AI risks.

- **Use AI risk management tools:** There are AI risk management tools that can help companies to identify and mitigate AI risks.

- **Partner with experts:** There are companies that specialize in AI risk management. These companies can provide guidance and support in developing and implementing effective AI risk management programs.

- **Monitoring AI risks:** After evaluating the AI risks, they are continuously monitored with any changes tracked and appropriate measures taken to mitigate them.

- **Reporting AI risks:** The results of the AI risk monitoring process are regularly reported to management ensuring informed decisions on managing AI risks.

WHY IT MATTERS?

Implementing AI risk monitoring is crucial for companies as it helps them safeguard against potential negative impacts related to AI. It empowers them to use AI responsibly and effectively making it a vital aspect of their operations. AI risk monitoring is an ongoing process since AI technology evolves leading to changes in risks. Thus, companies continually monitor and manage AI risks.

Benefits of AI risk monitoring include:

- **Reduced AI risk:** Continuously monitoring and managing AI risks allows companies to lower the chances of AI-related problems occurring. This protection helps prevent financial losses, damage to reputation, and other harmful outcomes.

- **Increased trust:** By consistently monitoring and managing AI risks, companies can build trust with their customers, employees, and other stakeholders. This trust-building fosters a positive reputation, which helps in attracting and retaining customers, employees, and investors.

AI AUDITING

AI auditing is a new way to make sure that AI systems are working properly and safely. In New York, there are laws that require companies to do AI auditing especially for automated AI systems used in hiring humans. The ISO 19011-2018 provides guidelines on how to do a risk-based audit.

WHAT IS THE RISK?

AI systems are often opaque meaning that it can be difficult to understand how they work. This can pose an AI risk to enterprise knowledge. If an AI system is used to make decisions and the risk-based decisions are not transparent, it can be difficult to understand why the risk-based decisions were made. This can make it difficult for the enterprise to learn from its mistakes.

Implementing AI risk reviews is crucial for companies as it helps them safeguard against potential negative impacts related to AI. By staying vigilant and proactive in managing AI risks, enterprises can use AI responsibly and with confidence.

WHAT ARE RISK-CONTROL EXAMPLES

AI risk management audit involves checking how a company is managing the risks with their AI systems. Here are the steps typically involved:

- **Reviewing AI risk management policies and procedures:** The auditor looks at the company's rules and guidelines for managing AI risks to make sure they cover everything and are up-to-date.

- **Assessing AI risk management practices:** The auditor checks if the company's processes for managing AI risks are effective and actually work in reducing those risks.

- **Interviewing AI risk management stakeholders:** The auditor talks to the humans involved in managing AI risks to get their opinions on how it is being done.

- **Reviewing and test AI data:** The auditor looks at the data that was used to train the AI system to see if it is appropriate and reliable.

- **Analyzing AI risk management data:** The auditor studies the data related to AI risk management to see if there are any trends or patterns that suggest the company's approach might not be effective.

- **Reporting the findings:** The auditor shares the results of the audit with the company's leadership, so they know how their AI risk management is working and if any changes are needed.

- **Take action on audit findings:** Address any issues or gaps identified in the audit by implementing new policies, training employees, or making other changes to the AI risk management program.

WHY IT MATTERS?

AI risk management audits are vital for a company's AI risk management program. By conducting AI risk management audits, companies can safeguard from potential negative consequences of AI. These audits help ensure that AI systems are used responsibly and ethically, protecting both the company and the users of AI technology.

AI VERIFICATION AND VALIDATION

Verification and validation are methods used to ensure that AI systems work correctly and meet human needs. Verification checks if the system meets its intended requirements, while validation ensures it meets what humans actually need.

WHAT IS THE RISK?

Machine learning (ML) models are hard to understand because they learn from massive amounts of data and the connections between data and their risk-based decisions are not always obvious. An ML model trained to identify cats in pictures might do it accurately, but it is challenging for regular humans to explain how it does that. The model might look for features like whiskers or ears but humans might not know which features are the most important.

This lack of understanding makes it tricky to validate ML models as humans cannot be sure if they are working as intended. It impacts trust in the models as if humans do not know how they work, humans might not trust them to make the right decisions.

To make ML models understandable humans can use explainable AI techniques, which explain how the models arrive at their risk-based decisions. Also providing transparency by sharing details about the data, algorithms, and performance of the model can make it trustworthy.

WHAT ARE AI RISK-CONTROL EXAMPLES?

If the validation process for AI systems is not adequate, it can lead to various risk-control problems when the system is deployed for use. Deployment is when the system becomes available to humans. Issues that arise due to improper deployment configuration include:

- **Accidental regressions:** When a new version of the system introduces errors that were not present in the previous version.

- **Unintended consequences:** The system's performance degrades over time due to changes in the environment or the data it is trained on.

- **Degradation in quality, reliability, or safety:** The system may not meet the needs of its users properly.

- **Resource problems:** The system is not properly configured to use the necessary resources like memory, computation, network storage, redundancy, or load balancing.

- **Performance problems:** The system does not function as expected.
- **Security problems:** The system is not properly configured to protect its data or humans.

WHY IT MATTERS?

Properly validating and deploying AI systems is crucial to avoid these problems and ensure that AI technology works as intended, meets human needs, performs well, and is secure. It helps build trust in AI and reduces the risk of negative impacts.

AI RISK TRACEABILITY

Being accountable and responsible in AI implementation can prevent negative impacts and build trust in AI systems.

WHAT IS THE RISK?

Tracking the use of AI systems by customers and external users is difficult. This is because there is intellectual property, contractual, or market restrictions that prevent companies from tracking how AI systems are used.

System accountability is about holding a human responsible for the risk-based decisions and actions of an AI system. When the system involves AI, it is challenging to assign accountability because AI systems can make risk-based decisions on their own leading to unexpected outcomes.

In the past when humans made risk-based decisions, they could be held accountable for their choices. With AI systems, it is not always clear who is held responsible when something goes wrong.

WHAT ARE AI RISK-CONTROL EXAMPLES?

It is important to track how the systems are performing and whether they are meeting the enterprise's objectives, which involves AI risk management and risk-control record keeping.

Companies can assure that their AI risk management records are accurate and complete. When companies use AI systems, it is essential to monitor how the systems are performing and whether they align with the company's objectives. This process is known as AI risk management record-keeping.

Tracking how customers are using AI systems can be challenging due to intellectual property, contractual, or market restrictions that limit companies from doing so. Despite these challenges, companies make efforts to track the use of AI systems by customers and external users. This information helps companies identify potential problems with the AI systems and ensure they are used in a safe and accountable manner.

An AI risk management record includes crucial information such as the AI system's name, description, the methodology used for assessing risks, the intended use of the AI system, details of the humans and companies involved in the risk assessment, terms of reference, assessment date, and the status of the risk assessment including any changes made since the initial assessment. This information allows companies to track the AI system's performance, ensure it meets their needs, and identify and mitigate potential issues.

Regulators are currently working on finding solutions to this problem. Here are examples of how companies can track the use of AI systems:

- **Be aware of the relevant AI legislation:** Understanding the laws related to AI can help determine who is accountable for the risk-based decisions and actions of the AI system.

- **Develop clear policies and procedures for using AI systems:** Creating guidelines that prioritize transparency, explainability, and fairness can help ensure accountable AI use.

- **Regularly monitor and audit the AI system:** Monitoring the system can help identify potential issues and allow corrective actions to be taken.

- **Establish a fair process for handling complaints related to the AI system:** Having a transparent and impartial complaint response process can provide compensation for any harm caused by the system.

- **Conduct user surveys:** These surveys help companies understand how customers are using AI systems and identify potential issues.

- **Monitor social media:** Social media can provide valuable insights into how humans use AI systems.

- **Track data usage:** Companies can monitor how much data the AI systems are using, which can help identify potential problems.

WHY IT MATTERS?

Companies should keep the AI risk management record in a secure location, update it regularly, and make it accessible to relevant stakeholders. By maintaining accurate and complete AI risk management records, companies can be confident that their AI systems are used responsibly and effectively, benefitting both the company and its users.

AI MAINTAINABILITY

Maintainability is about how to make changes to an AI system. This is crucial because AI systems are used in critical applications like self-driving cars and medical diagnosis systems. If something goes wrong with an AI system, it is essential to fix it quickly.

WHAT IS THE RISK?

Maintainability is a challenge for AI systems. This is because they are trained on vast amounts of data, which are complex and difficult to modify without impacting the system's performance. It is important for developers to take steps to mitigate the AI risks with verification, validation, deployment, and maintenance.

WHAT ARE AI RISK-CONTROL EXAMPLES?

To improve maintainability of AI systems, developers adopt certain risk-control practices:

- **Using a modular approach to development:** Breaking down the AI system into smaller, independent parts makes it easier to change specific components without disrupting the whole system.

- **Implementing a version control system:** This tool allows developers to track and manage changes made to the AI system. If necessary, they go back to previous versions if an issue arises.

- **Testing thoroughly:** The importance of thorough testing before deploying any changes to the AI system to ensure it functions correctly.

- **Using a Process:** Having a well-defined process for handling problems that arise with the AI system, so issues are addressed promptly and efficiently.

- **Using a rigorous verification and validation process:** This includes testing the system thoroughly and identifying and fixing any errors.

- **Using a secure deployment configuration:** This includes configuring the system to use the resources that it needs and to protect its data and its users.

- **Providing ongoing maintenance:** This includes ensuring the system is up to date with the latest security patches and updates.

WHY IT MATTERS?

Improving the maintainability of AI systems helps developers address problems quickly and keep the systems up-to-date with new requirements. This ensures that AI technology remains reliable and performs well in critical applications, benefiting both developers and end-users.

FREQUENCY OF AI FAILURES

Frequency is a measure of how often something happens in a given period of time. In AI, frequency is used to analyze data and identify patterns. Frequency analysis is used to identify trends in customer behavior, detect fraud, or predict when a machine is likely to fail.

WHAT IS THE RISK?

In AI, there are techniques to analyze frequency data. One popular method is using a frequency distribution, which shows how frequently different values occur in a dataset. Another approach is using a histogram, which is a visual representation of a frequency distribution.

WHAT ARE AI RISK-CONTROL EXAMPLES?

Frequency analysis is a powerful risk-control tool for AI systems. By understanding the frequency of events, AI systems make risk-based decisions and take effective actions in various fields. Here are examples of how frequency analysis is applied in AI:

- **Natural language processing:** Analyzing word and phrase frequency in a text helps improve tasks like machine translation and text classification.

- **Computer vision:** Identifying the frequency of different features in an image enhances tasks such as object detection and face recognition.

- **Speech recognition:** Analyzing sound frequency in a speech recording improves tasks like transcribing audio recordings and controlling devices with voice commands.

- **Robotics:** Understanding movement frequency in a robot helps in path planning and collision avoidance.

WHY IT MATTERS?

Frequency analysis is crucial in improving AI system performance. By understanding event frequencies, AI systems make informed decisions and execute actions efficiently.

Using frequency analysis in AI brings several benefits:

- **Understand patterns:** It helps AI systems understand patterns and trends, leading to smarter risk-based, decision-making; accurate predictions; and improved overall performance. This ensures that AI technologies are effective and useful in various real-world applications.

- **Improve accuracy:** Frequency analysis improves the accuracy of AI systems by identifying patterns in data that would otherwise be difficult to see.

- **Reduce costs:** Frequency analysis reduces the costs of AI systems by identifying areas where optimization is possible.

- **Increase speed:** Frequency analysis increases the speed of AI systems by identifying patterns that are used to predict future events.

- **Improve risk-based, decision-making:** Frequency analysis improves the decision-making process by providing insights into the frequency of events.

AI RISK REPORTING

Recording and reporting are essential processes that enterprises perform regularly to ensure the effectiveness of their AI risk treatment plan.

WHAT IS THE RISK?

AI risk reporting is the process of communicating the risks with AI to stakeholders. It is an important part of any enterprise's AI risk management program. By tracking the plan's performance, an organization makes informed decisions on managing AI risk effectively. Recording and reporting are crucial for effective AI risk management. These processes provide insights into the AI risk treatment plan's progress and help optimize the AI system's performance, making it reliable and trustworthy.

WHAT ARE AI RISK-CONTROL EXAMPLES?

After implementing an AI risk-control treatment plan and risk assurance, it is crucial to monitor its progress. This is where recording and reporting come in. These processes involve documenting and communicating the following:

- Types of AI risks that the enterprise faces.
- Likelihood and consequence of each AI risk.
- Steps that the enterprise is taking to mitigate AI risks.
- Outcomes of the AI risk treatment plan.
- Any modifications made to the plan.
- AI system's performance.
- Newly identified AI risks arising from using the AI system.
- Changes in the enterprise's AI risk appetite due to using the AI system.

AI Conformity Assessment

- Involvement of stakeholders in the process.

- Accuracy and completeness of the recorded data.

- Timeliness of the reports.

WHY IT MATTERS?

When companies use AI systems, they regularly evaluate their AI risk management activities to ensure that they are still effective. This evaluation involves analyzing the impact of any changes made to the AI system such as modifications to its goals, how it is used, or its performance. If these changes could impact AI risk, the company takes measures to mitigate those risks. These measures might involve updating AI risk treatment plans, implementing new safety measures, or adjusting the company's tolerance for AI risks.

KEY POINTS

- EU AIA uses the conformity assessment scheme to determine compliance with its statutes.

- Conformity assessment is a process for determining if the AI systems can fulfill the requirements in a standard, guidelines, or best practices.

- There are many factors to determining AI conformity assessment such as the context, purpose, humans, and data of the system.

- AI accountability is the ability to explain the risk-based decisions made by the AI system.

- AI assurance is the ability to determine trust in the risk-based decisions made by the AI system.

- AI auditing is a method to determine assurance.

AI FUTURES

WHAT IS THE KEY IDEA IN THIS CHAPTER?

Because AI is constantly evolving, it is difficult to predict how it will be used in the future. This means that governments and companies need to be flexible and adaptable when it comes to managing AI risks. It is critical to assure that AI is developed and used so it minimizes the AI risks and maximizes the benefits. Because of the many AI changes, this book will probably be updated every six months.

COMPLEX ENVIRONMENTS

Complex environments are challenging for AI systems because there are many different factors that can impact the behavior of the system. It is difficult to identify all of the possible situations that the system might encounter and it is difficult to collect enough data to train the system to handle these situations.

WHAT IS THE RISK?

Additional AI risks arise in complex environments because the system is not able to handle all the possible situations that it might encounter. This could lead to the system making mistakes, which could cause harm.

It is important to consider the degree to which the AI system environment is understood before deploying the system in a complex environment. This will identify potential AI risks and take steps to mitigate them.

AI risks that occur in complex environments include:

- **Identifying possible situations:** Experts in the field and simulations help brainstorm and envision potential scenarios the AI system might encounter.

- **Collecting enough data:** To train the AI system properly, data from historical records, simulations, and real-world observations is gathered.

- **Designing for robustness:** Creating the AI system to be resilient and able to handle unexpected situations using techniques like fault tolerance and anomaly detection.

- **Thorough testing:** Before deploying in a complex environment, extensively test the AI system in various settings including simulated and real-world environments.

WHAT ARE AI RISK-CONTROL EXAMPLES?

AI systems face challenges in complex environments because there are many factors that influence how the system behaves. It is hard to predict the different situations the system might encounter and collect enough data to train it effectively. In complex environments, additional AI risks arise because the system is not prepared to handle possible situations. This could lead to mistakes that might harm humans or property.

Before deploying an AI system in a complex environment, it is crucial to thoroughly understand the environment and design appropriate risk-controls. This means identifying potential AI risks and taking steps to address them.

WHY IT MATTERS?

Understanding and addressing the risks of complex environments are crucial for the safe and effective use of AI systems, avoiding potential harm and enhancing their reliability.

CONTROLLED AI ENVIRONMENTS

Complete understanding of a simple environment means that the AI system knows everything about the environment including the possible states that the environment is in. This is only possible for simple, predictable, or controlled environments. This is often impossible.

WHAT IS THE RISK?

To put it simply, when an AI system understands its environment including the different situations it can be in. This is usually only possible in simple, predictable, or controlled

Future AI Challenges 221

environments. In complex, unpredictable, or uncontrolled environments, the AI system might not know everything and AI engineers call this 'partial understanding. So, AI developers mitigate AI risks with only partial understanding of an environment and assure that their AI systems are safe and reliable.

When the AI system only partially understands its environment, it cannot predict the different situations it might face. This uncertainty is a source of AI risk and it needs to be considered when designing AI systems for complex environments.

WHAT ARE AI RISK-CONTROL EXAMPLES?

To reduce the risks with only a partial understanding of an environment, developers should consider additional risk-controls including:

- Design the AI system to be robust and handle unexpected situations by using techniques like fault tolerance and anomaly detection.

- Test the AI system extensively in various environments including simulated and real-world scenarios.

- Create a plan for how to handle unexpected situations outlining steps for identifying and responding to them.

AI system developers understand their environment to operate safely and effectively. If the environment is complex or unpredictable, the AI system might not understand it leading to potential mistakes that could harm humans or property.

WHY IT MATTERS?

By addressing the AI risks related to partial understanding of an environment, developers ensure that their AI systems are safe, reliable, and equipped to handle real-world challenges.

AI SYSTEM LIFECYCLES

System lifecycle issues are AI risks that arise at any stage in the development and use of an AI system.

WHAT IS THE RISK?

System lifecycle issues refer to AI risks that occur at any stage of developing and using an AI system. These risks arise due to various reasons including using inappropriate methods or insufficient processes, inadequate testing, changes in the environment, or human errors made by developers, users, or operators.

These AI risks lead to various problems such as system failures causing harm to humans or property, data breaches resulting in the loss of sensitive information, financial losses if the system does not perform as expected, and reputational damage if the system is misused or found to be unreliable.

WHAT ARE AI RISK-CONTROL EXAMPLES?

To mitigate the AI risks with system lifecycle issues, developers and humans can take the following risk-control steps:

- Use appropriate methods and processes including the right tools and best practices.

- Thoroughly test the system in various environments both simulated and real-world.

- Continuously monitor the system's performance after deployment and make necessary changes.

- Train humans on how to use the system safely and effectively, and how to identify and report problems.

WHY IT MATTERS?

AI systems are developed and should be used with great care. If improper methods or processes are used or if the system is not thoroughly tested, it might not function correctly. This could lead to serious issues such as system failures, data breaches, and financial losses. It is crucial to manage AI risks in every stage of an AI system's life cycle to ensure their safety and reliability.

DECOMMISSIONING AI

Companies that stop using an AI system or a component of an AI system loses information or risk-based decision-making expertise that was provided by the system.

WHAT IS THE RISK?

An enterprise that stops using an AI system that was used to make predictions about sales could lose the ability to make accurate predictions about sales. If a new system is used to replace a decommissioned system, the way in which an enterprise processes information and makes risk-based decisions can change.

WHAT ARE AI RISK-CONTROL EXAMPLES?

To mitigate the risks with decommissioning AI systems, companies can take the following risk-control steps:

- **Understand the requirements of the new use case:** Before reusing an AI system, companies thoroughly understand the needs and demands of the new use case, including the required precision and available data.

- **Test the AI system in the new use case:** Before deploying an AI system in a new use case, companies conduct rigorous testing to ensure that it meets the specific requirements of the new scenario.

- **Monitor the AI system in the new use case:** After deploying an AI system in a new use case, continuous monitoring is essential to ensure that it performs as expected and meets the desired outcomes.

- **Plan for decommissioning:** Companies plan for the decommissioning of AI systems by identifying the information and expertise that will be lost and have a plan in place to replace or compensate for that loss.

WHY IT MATTERS?

It is crucial for companies to be aware of the risks with reusing or decommissioning AI systems. Proper planning, testing, and monitoring are essential to ensure a smooth transition and avoid potential disruptions in information processing and decision-making.

KEY POINTS

- It is difficult to predict AI futures, because AI is constantly evolving.

- AI in complex environments is very difficult to control and even predict its behavior.

- AI if possible should be designed and deployed in a controlled environment.

- AI is developed through a system lifecycle. Risk-controls should be designed for each phase of the lifecycle.

- Decommissioning AI is critical because its risk-based, decision making can degrade due to change assumptions and context.

Index

A

accountabilities, 52, 57, 58, 67, 73

accountability, 22, 26, 37, 38, 62, 74, 79, 83, 94, 99, 116, 120, 121, 141, 147, 177, 184, 200, 201, 202, 203, 204, 211, 217

accountable, 8, 11, 22, 23, 26, 33, 35, 38, 61, 62, 79, 82, 84, 85, 86, 93, 94, 95, 98, 106, 109, 117, 132, 155, 161, 184, 188, 190, 201, 205, 210, 211

accuracy, 53, 55, 69

AI, 1, 3, 5, 7, 8, 9, 10, 11, 12, 13, 14, 15, 17, 18, 19, 20, 21, 22, 23, 24, 25, 26, 27, 28, 29, 30, 31, 32, 33, 34, 35, 36, 37, 38, 39, 41, 42, 43, 44, 45, 46, 47, 48, 50, 51, 52, 53, 54, 56, 58, 61, 62, 66, 68, 71, 72, 76, 77, 78, 79, 80, 81, 82, 83, 84, 85, 86, 87, 88, 89, 90, 91, 92, 93, 94, 95, 96, 97, 98, 99, 100, 101, 102, 103, 104, 105, 106, 107, 108, 109, 110, 111, 112, 113, 114, 115, 116, 117, 118, 119, 120, 121, 122, 123, 124, 125, 126, 127, 128, 129, 131, 132, 133, 134, 135, 136, 137, 138, 139, 140, 141, 143, 144, 145, 146, 147, 148, 149, 150, 151, 152, 153, 154, 155, 156, 157, 158, 159, 160, 161, 162, 163, 164, 165, 166, 167, 169, 170, 171, 172, 173, 174, 175, 176, 177, 178, 179, 180, 181, 182, 183, 184, 185, 186, 187, 188, 189, 190, 191, 192, 193, 194, 195, 196, 197, 198, 199, 200, 201, 202, 203, 204, 205, 206, 207, 208, 209, 210, 211, 212, 213, 214, 215, 216, 217, 219, 220, 221, 222, 223, 224, 226

AI Bill of Rights, 12, 37

AI governance, 8, 43, 117, 118, 128

AI risk management, 7, 9, 20, 27, 31, 36, 37, 39, 41, 54, 81, 105, 109, 110, 112, 113, 114, 115, 116, 118, 119, 120, 121, 122, 129, 132, 134, 139, 140, 149, 152, 165, 170, 171, 173, 178, 179, 180, 183, 186, 189, 190, 191, 192, 193, 194, 197, 204, 206, 207, 208, 209, 211, 212, 215, 216

algorithmic bias, 24

algorithms, 24, 62, 81, 87, 91, 92, 95, 102, 103, 157, 158, 159, 210

ambiguity, 58

architecture, 50, 57

assurance, 43, 49, 54, 57, 69, 72, 74

attributes, 48

audits, 192

automated tasks, 144

automation, 25

B

best available information, 53, 54, 55, 59

Board of Directors, 47, 56, 74

business model, 44, 46, 52, 65

business objectives, 73, 74

C

cascading, 68, 69

change management, 66

ChatGPT, 10, 11

clear responsibility, 201

climate change, 18, 19

complex environments, 219

complexity, 58, 67

compliance, 43, 44

computer vision, 157, 214

conformity assessment, 9, 43, 57, 197, 204, 205, 217

consequence, 46, 69, 70

consistency, 53

consultation, 64, 65, 66, 68, 70

context, 8, 43, 44, 45, 46, 47, 49, 50, 52, 53, 55, 56, 59, 64, 66, 67, 69, 70, 71, 73, 74, 78, 79, 103, 111, 118, 123, 131, 133, 134, 135, 136, 137, 138, 139, 141, 148, 149, 150, 152, 153, 167, 186, 187, 199, 200, 206, 217

continual improvement, 57

continuous change, 140

control, 45, 46, 52, 53, 57, 71, 72

cyberattacks, 33

D

data complexity, 140

data poisoning, 88, 198

data quality, 32

decision-making, 3, 45, 47, 135, 160

dependency, 71

design, 41, 42, 43, 49, 50, 51, 57, 66, 72, 74

discrimination, 25, 90

due professional care, 49

dynamic, 52

enterprise governance, 84

enterprise level, 49, 68, 70, 73

ethical considerations, 177

EU AI Act, 13, 204

evaluation, 70, 71

event, 69

evidence based, decision-making, 54

executive leadership, 71

executive management, 63, 75, 77, 108, 110, 113

explainability, 21, 37, 76, 92, 94, 95, 96, 98, 99, 131, 201, 203, 212

external risk sources, 33

F

fairness, 8, 10, 37, 38, 43, 62, 79, 83, 87, 93, 99, 106, 120, 121, 123, 125, 127, 177, 201, 203, 206, 212

framework, 49, 50, 51, 52, 53, 55, 58, 64, 65, 66, 67, 68, 70, 71, 72, 73, 74

fraud, 12, 24, 29, 158, 214

frequency, 214, 215

G

GM, 56

governance, 43, 44, 46, 57

government regulations, 138

H

harassment, 90

hardware maintenance, 32

hazards, 32, 33, 34, 69, 74

human error, 32

human rights, 84

humans, 7, 10, 15, 19, 21, 38, 85, 92, 143, 144

I

identity theft, 90

inclusive, 51

inclusiveness, 51, 84

Infrastructure, 49, 126, 153

interdependencies, 68

interest parties, 65, 71

interested parties, 52, 55, 56, 65, 66

International Organization for Standardization, 75, 112, 122

ISO 26000, 84, 85

ISO 31000, 41, 42, 43, 48, 49, 50, 52

ISO 31000, 5, 7, 8, 20, 41, 42, 43, 45, 48, 49, 51, 53, 55, 56, 57, 58, 61, 63, 64, 65, 66, 67, 68, 70, 71, 72, 73, 74, 75, 76, 77, 110, 111, 112, 113, 114, 128, 149, 150

ISO 42001, 76

ISO/IEC 23894:2023, 122

K

Key Performance Indicators, 47, 57

Key Risk Indicators, 47, 57

KPI, 53, 57, 58, 65, 73

KRI, 47, 53, 57, 58, 65, 73

lack of accountability, 26, 147

likelihood, 8, 26, 63, 64, 69, 70, 80, 83, 90, 111, 120, 121, 139, 143, 146, 147, 151, 152, 155, 156, 157, 158, 159, 160, 165, 167, 170, 177, 183, 184, 185, 187, 191, 192, 193, 206, 216

LISP, 11

M

machine learning, 209

maintainability, 8, 79, 213

management system, 43, 57, 58

medical diagnosis, 19

model complexity, 140

model hacking, 24, 147

model inversion, 198

model stealing, 88, 198

monitor and review, 170, 178, 205

monitoring, 57, 72, 73, 74

N

natural language processing, 157, 214

O

OpenAI, 18, 101, 102

Operational Risk Committee, 56

opportunities, 19, 20, 24, 36, 37, 44, 71, 74, 93, 95, 105, 122, 126, 137, 138, 143, 166, 176, 185, 188, 193

P

physical attack, 198

physical environment, 32

physical tampering, 162

policies, 136, 192, 201, 203

positive risks, 185

principles, 5, 41

privacy, 8, 11, 25, 26, 35, 62, 79, 82, 83, 86, 89, 90, 91, 95, 97, 98, 99, 107, 117, 123, 124, 125, 127, 128, 131, 132, 161, 177

procedures, 192, 201, 203

programmatic, 49, 70, 73

project, 49, 70, 73

Q

qualitative likelihood, 158

quantitative likelihood, 158

R

RBDM, 20, 26, 47, 51, 54, 57, 58, 69

RBPS, 20, 26, 47, 51, 54, 57, 58, 69, 73

regulatory environment, 173, 178

reliability, 55, 69

residual risk, 71, 72, 73, 175, 182

resources, 51, 52, 67

responsibilities, 52, 57, 67, 73

review, 72

risk, 1, 18, 26, 31, 36, 37, 41, 46, 49, 51, 52, 61, 67, 68, 70, 71, 83, 105, 111, 112, 119, 120, 121, 139, 143, 145, 146, 147, 150, 152, 155, 156, 158, 160, 161, 162, 165, 169, 171, 172, 173, 175, 177, 179, 180, 183, 186, 188, 189, 190, 193, 206, 210, 215

risk acceptance, 189, 190, 191

risk analysis, 68, 69, 70, 105, 155, 156, 157

risk appetite, 8, 9, 45, 47, 49, 51, 52, 53, 65, 70, 71, 72, 73, 74, 111, 117, 169, 171, 172, 176, 179, 182, 183, 216

risk assessment, 8, 67, 68, 74, 111, 135, 143, 146, 150, 151, 152, 154, 155, 156, 158, 162, 163, 165, 167, 170, 206, 211

risk averse, 174

Risk Based Decision Making, 53, 55, 71

Risk Based Problem Solving, 65, 67

risk consequences, 160

risk control, 51, 74, 183, 191, 193, 196

risk criteria, 65, 66, 74

risk evaluation, 67, 70, 156

risk identification, 67, 68

risk management, 41, 42, 43, 45, 46, 47, 48, 49, 50, 51, 52, 53, 55, 56, 57, 58, 64, 65, 66, 67, 68, 70, 71, 72, 73, 74

risk management framework, 8, 27, 31, 41, 48, 49, 50, 51, 53, 55, 56, 58, 61, 62, 63, 64, 65, 66, 74, 75, 76, 77, 80, 109, 110, 113, 117, 176, 179, 183, 185, 196

risk management plan, 27, 57, 65, 115, 120, 121, 129, 170, 194, 206

risk management policy, 109, 110, 113, 119, 120

risk management process, 20, 27, 31, 42, 43, 49, 64, 65, 66, 67, 72, 73, 112, 113, 114, 134, 139, 140, 149, 183, 186, 191

risk objectives, 98, 99

risk owner, 105

risk registers, 156

risk resilience, 179, 180, 182

risk retention, 189, 190

risk sensitivity, 69

risk sources, 31

risk tolerance, 47, 51

risk treatment, 8, 71, 72, 183, 186, 187, 196, 215, 216

risk workshops, 156

risk-averse, 172, 173, 174, 177, 178, 188

risk-based auditing, 202, 203

risk-based decision-making, 54, 65, 70, 73

risk-based, problem solving, 26

risk-control, 21, 44, 47, 48, 50, 52, 53, 54, 56, 58

risk-taking, 174

robotic surgery, 28

robustness, 8, 79, 92, 99, 220

robustness, 91

S

safety, 8, 12, 13, 14, 26, 56, 79, 83, 88, 89, 99, 101, 123, 124, 125, 151, 154, 157, 160, 166, 174, 185, 200, 204, 210, 216, 223

security risks, 10, 62, 81, 85, 87, 88, 95, 131

self-driving automobiles, 28

software maintenance, 32

software vulnerabilities, 25, 147, 198

speech recognition, 214

stakeholders, 36, 51, 86, 92, 93, 97, 98, 106, 206

stock market, 19

supply chain, 56

sustainability, 144

system bias, 145, 148, 159

system failure, 34, 145, 148

system misuse, 34, 35, 145, 148, 159

T

technological environment, 138

threat modeling, 62, 151

threats, 68, 69

tolerance, 72, 73

tone at the top, 43

transactional level, 49, 68

transparency, 8, 14, 22, 25, 26, 37, 38, 51, 61, 76, 79, 83, 95, 98, 99, 106, 120, 121, 147, 177, 201, 203, 210, 212

treatment, 50, 51, 52, 64, 65, 70, 71, 72

treatment options, 71

trust, 7, 8, 10, 11, 12, 15, 24, 36, 37, 38, 79, 82, 92, 93, 94, 95, 101, 104, 106, 124, 125, 132, 147, 152, 154, 166, 173, 179, 180, 184, 186, 193, 195, 200, 202, 203, 204, 206, 207, 209, 210, 217, 226

trust me, 1, 10

trustworthiness, 81

U

uncertainty, 7, 17, 18, 19, 20, 21, 22, 39, 45, 46, 50, 52, 53, 54, 58, 67, 69, 111, 131, 133, 157, 158, 221

unintended consequences, 80, 83, 128, 151, 152

V

Value, 42, 43

Verification and validation, 209

volatility, 58

VUCA, 58

VUCAN, 3, 17

vulnerability, 159, 188, 197

W

Working It, 3

Endnotes

[1] Proactive, Preventive, Predictive, Preemptive® and Architect, Design, Deploy Assure® are registered trademarks of Quality + Engineering.

[2] Building Trust in AI,' IBM, https://www.ibm.com/watson/advantage-reports/future-of-artificial-intelligence/building-trust-in-ai.html, 2023.

[3] Administration Secure Voluntary Commitments From Leading AI Companies to Manage Risks Posed by AI,' White House, July 22, 2023.

[4] 'The Roadmap to an Effective AI Assurance System,' UK, December 8, 2021.

[5] 'Can humans Trust AI,' Caltech Science Exchange, https://scienceexchange.caltech.edu/topics/artificial-intelligence-research/trustworthy-ai, July 2023.

[6] 'Actors and Writers Aren't the Only Ones Worried About AI, New Polling Shows,' LA Times, August 6, 2023.

[7] Excellence and trust in artificial intelligence,' EU, https://commission.europa.eu/strategy-and-policy/priorities-2019-2024/europe-fit-digital-age/excellence-and-trust-artificial-intelligence_en#latest, July 30, 2023.

[8] Excellence and trust in artificial intelligence,' EU, https://commission.europa.eu/strategy-and-policy/priorities-2019-2024/europe-fit-digital-age/excellence-and-trust-artificial-intelligence_en#latest, July 30, 2023.

[9] Excellence and trust in artificial intelligence,' EU, https://commission.europa.eu/strategy-and-policy/priorities-2019-2024/europe-fit-digital-age/excellence-and-trust-artificial-intelligence_en#latest, July 30, 2023.

[10] Excellence and trust in artificial intelligence,' EU, https://commission.europa.eu/strategy-and-policy/priorities-2019-2024/europe-fit-digital-age/excellence-and-trust-artificial-intelligence_en#latest, July 30, 2023.

[11] 'Trust in Artificial Intelligence, ' KPMG & University of Queensland, 2023.

[12] 'Up To 80 Percent of Workers Could See Jobs Impacted by AI,' NY Post, March 26, 2023.

[13] What Are the Risks Of Using AI in Business?' Financial Times, July 19, 2023.

[14] NIST AIRMF Presentation, Elham Tabassi, July 2023.

[15] NIST AIRMF Presentation, Elham Tabassi, July 2023.

[16] Wikipedia, 'Uncertainty', 2015.

[17] Dictionary.com, 'Uncertainty', 2015.

[18] Merriam Webster, 'Uncertainty', 2015.

[19] 'Can You Trust AI: Here's Why You Shouldn't,' Bruce Schneier and Nathan Sanders, *The Conversation*, July 20, 2023.

[20] Benefits and Risks of AI,' Capers Jones, *CERM Risk Insights*, July 23, 2023.

[21] 'The Influence of AI on Trust in Human Interaction,' Science News, may 8, 2023.

[22] Benefits and Risks of AI,' Capers Jones, CERM Risk Insights, July 23, 2023.

[23] 'What Are the Risks Of Using AI in Business?' Financial Times, July 19, 2023.
[24] Building Trust in AI,' IBM, https://www.ibm.com/watson/advantage-reports/future-of-artificial-intelligence/building-trust-in-ai.html, 2023.
[25] Building Trust in AI,' IBM, https://www.ibm.com/watson/advantage-reports/future-of-artificial-intelligence/building-trust-in-ai.html, 2023.
[26] General Motors Company Risk Committee Charter, 2014, Web.
[27] 'How ISO/IEC 42001 Guides Organizations Toward Trustworthy AI,' AI Standards Hub website, August 23, 2023.
[28] No One Should Trust Artificial Intelligence,' Our World, Joanna Bryson, November 14, 2014.
[29] Addressing AI's Biggest Problem Trust, Suresh Chintada, Forbes, October 25, 2021.
[30] 'Salesforce Survey Flags AI Trust Gap Between Enterprises and Customers,' *VentureBeat*, August 28, 2023.

[31] 'Socially Responsible AI Algorithms:Issues, Purposes, and Challenges,' Lu Cheng, Kush Varshney, Huan Liu, *Journal of AI Research*, August, 2021.

[32] '7 AI Companies Vow To Guard Against AI Risks,' *Arkansas Democrat Gazette*, July 21, 2023

Printed in Great Britain
by Amazon